Books from the Attic
Treasures from an Irish Childhood

About Alice Taylor's other books

To School through the Fields
'One of the most richly evocative and moving portraits of
childhood ever written.' *Boston Globe*
'A delightful evocation of Irishness and of the author's deep-rooted
love of "the very fields of home" ... with its rituals and local characters'
Publishers Weekly

Do You Remember?
'magical ... reading the book, I felt a faint ache in my heart ... I find
myself longing for those days ... this book is important social history ...
remembering our past is important. Alice Taylor has given us a handbook
for survival. In fact, it is essential reading' *Irish Independent*

For more books by Alice Taylor, see www.obrien.ie

Alice Taylor went to school in the 1940s and 1950s when the selection of books on the school curriculum cultivated in children an awareness of the natural world in which they lived, while, at the same time, nurturing an appreciation of the wonder of the written word. The poems and stories in these books formed a mental nucleus which spawned her future thinking, and the words of the poems in particular stayed with her for the rest of her life.

Other books by Alice Taylor

To School through the Fields
A Cocoon with a View
As Time Goes By
And Life Lights Up
The Women
Do You Remember?
Tea and Talk

See the O'Brien Press website
www.obrien.ie
for a full list

Books from the Attic

Treasures from an Irish Childhood

Alice Taylor

Photographs by Emma Byrne

BRANDON

First published 2020 by Brandon
An imprint of The O'Brien Press Ltd.
12 Terenure Road East, Rathgar,
Dublin 6, D06 HD27, Ireland.
Tel: +353 1 4923333 Fax: +353 1 4922777

Email: books@obrien.ie
Website: www.obrien.ie

The O'Brien Press is a member of Publishing Ireland.

ISBN: 978-1-78849-214-0

Cover and book design by Emma Byrne

10 9 8 7 6 5 4 3 2 1
23 22 21 20

Printed and bound in Drukarnia Skleniarz, Poland.
The paper used in this book is produced using pulp from
managed forests.

Published in:

DUBLIN
UNESCO
City of Literature

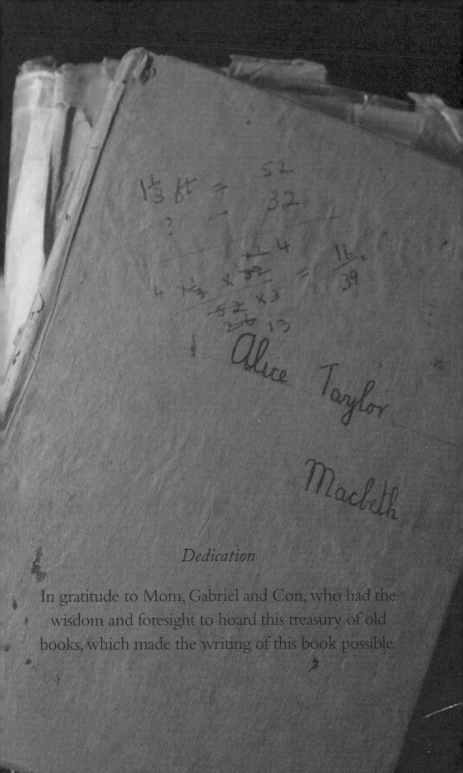

$1\frac{1}{3}$ ft $=$ $\frac{52}{32}$

$\frac{?}{}$

$4 \times \frac{}{} \times \frac{4}{52} = \frac{16}{39}$

$\frac{52 \times 3}{2 \times 6} \quad 13$

Alice Taylor

Macbeth

Dedication

In gratitude to Mom, Gabriel and Con, who had the
wisdom and foresight to hoard this treasury of old
books, which made the writing of this book possible.

SCHOOL AND COLLEGE SERIES.

Edited by Rev. T. A. FINLAY, M.A., F.R.U.I.

Fourth School Reader.

ADOPTED BY THE COMMISSIONERS OF NATIONAL EDUCATION.

180th THOUSAND.

James O'Neill

6/7/07

Wm O'Neill

FALLON & CO., LTD.,
SCHOOL PUBLISHERS,
DUBLIN AND BELFAST.

1905.

Contents

Chapter 1

A Hoarder's Haven

Welcome to my attic! A family of old friends lives up here. Over the years they crept silently up the steep, narrow stairs, gently eased open the creaking door and slipped in quietly. They made themselves comfortable and now have earned their right of residence. When my life downstairs was frantic with the demands of business and small children they reached down with welcoming arms and raised me up. Up here in the restful silence they fostered and encouraged my first tentative steps into the world of writing. These comforters were handed on to me by family hoarders who had cherished and loved them for decades. Now they are my protégés and I would like to introduce them to you, and you may be pleasantly surprised to be reunited with some long-forgotten friends, and hopefully make new ones.

My mother was a hoarder and kept all our schoolbooks. My husband Gabriel was another hoarder who kept his schoolbooks. My cousin Con, who became part of our family, was an extreme hoarder and brought all his old schoolbooks with him when he came to live in our house. So a deep drift of old schoolbooks was building up and would eventually swirl in my direction.

In the home place, my mother stored all our old schoolbooks up in a dark attic that was christened the 'black loft' because in those pre-electricity days only faint rays of light penetrated its dusty depths under the sloping roof of our old farmhouse. Gabriel stored his in a recess under the stairs, which he had cordoned off from our destructive offspring. You entered his mini library via a handmade little door secured with a bolt above child-level access. An adult gaining entry to this literary archive then had to genuflect and go on all-fours to reach the shelves in the furthest corners. Con stored his books under his bed and on shelves all around his bedroom, until the room resembled a kind of beehive of books. When these three much-loved family members climbed the library ladder to the heavenly book archives, I became the custodian of all these old schoolbooks.

My sister Phil sorted out our mother's collection of a lifetime, brought them from the home place and landed a large box of books on my kitchen table with the firm instructions: 'You look after these now.' We went through them with 'Ohs' and 'Ahs' of remembrance. In the box was a miscellaneous collection of moth-eaten, tattered and bat-tered-looking schoolbooks. Amongst them was a book that had belonged to our old neighbour Bill, who had gone to school with my father. It was somehow uncanny that here was a reminder of Bill, who, every night during our child-hood all those years ago, came down from his home on the hill behind our house and taught us our lessons. He was a Hans Christian Andersen who loved children and had the patience of Job, so he was the ideal teacher and we loved him dearly. He spent long hours teaching us our lessons; one night he spent over an hour patiently trying to drum the spelling of 'immediately' into my heedless head. All the books eventually found their way up into my attic with promises of: Some day, some day! Isn't life littered with good intentions!

For many years all these old books remained stored away in the attic, gathering dust. Occasionally when I was up there rummaging through miscellaneous abandoned objects looking for something else, I would come across one of them. Planning just a quick peep inside, I was still there half an hour later, steeped in memories. These impromptu sessions transported me back into the world of *To School through the Fields.*

That first peep into a book sometimes led to a search through others along the shelves, looking for another where a half-remembered poem or some lessons I half-recalled might be hidden. Having found that other book, the nearest chair was sought and a journey back down memory lane ensued. This sometimes provided a welcome break in a then busy schedule downstairs and there was deep satisfaction in these stolen moments.

There and then the promise would again be made that one day all these old schoolbooks would be gathered together and sorted out. I owed it to my mother, to Gabriel and to Con, who had all so carefully preserved them and entrusted their future to me. Unfortunately, it never happened. But lodged at the very back of my mind was the thought that one day when I too would climb the golden library ladder all these old books could well finish up in a skip! A terrible thought! But if I, who knew and loved the history of these books did nothing with them, how could I expect someone who had no nostalgic connection with them to do what I had failed to do? But after these episodes it was back on the conveyor belt of a busy life, which flattens us all. But sometimes life has a funny way of working things out in spite of us and as time evolves it comes up with its own solutions. And so it was with this collection of old schoolbooks.

On recent long car journeys, my grand-daughter Ellie, aged seven, and I are back-seat passengers, and these journeys invariably evolve into storytelling sessions. And one day I said to Ellie: 'I think that I have become your Gobán Saor.' 'Nana, what's a Gobán Saor?' she inquired.

Now, there are many stories about the Gobán Saor, I told her, but probably the correct one is that he was a very good mason who worked for free or very cheaply, was skilled at building, and always managed to get his due, whatever the circumstances. But my favourite story about him is this. And so I told her my version of the Gobán Saor story, in which he is a man who loved storytelling. She loved it.

Long, long ago there was a Gobán Saor who had a large kingdom and three sons. He had to make a big decision. He had to make up his mind to which of his three sons he would leave his kingdom. This was a very big decision. So one day he took the eldest son and some of his courtiers on a long, long journey and when they were all getting weary he asked his son: 'Son, shorten the road for me.' The son looked at him in surprise and protested: 'Father, how can I shorten the road for you? I cannot cut a bit off it.' So they continued on in silence.

The following day the king took his second son and as they walked along he said to the second son: 'Son, shorten the road for me.' And the second son made the same response, so they walked on in silence. When they came home that night the queen knew that the following day it would be the turn of the third and youngest son. This son was kind and wise and would make a good king, and she wanted him to inherit the kingdom. So that night she whispered a secret in his ear.

The next day as the father and son walked along, the father said to his youngest son: 'Shorten the road for me, son.' And the son began to tell his father a fascinating story to which the father and all the courtiers listened in awe. The time flew by and they never noticed the long journey and arrived at their destination in no time at all. And so the youngest son inherited the kingdom.

When Ellie heard this story she absorbed every last detail and demanded that it be retold many times, precisely as she had first heard it. The Gobán Saor led on to other old stories and she was completely fascinated by the stories, myths and legends that I had learnt in school. A visit back up to the attic was necessary to re-familiarise myself with these stories. Many had totally faded from my memory and rediscovering them was like meeting up with old friends. I decided now was the time to rescue the old books.

I gathered them all together into one long flat box, brought them downstairs and spread them out on the kitchen table. It was an old school reunion. At last all these old friends were back together. Many were tattered and torn from lots of grubby-fingered thumbing and years of dusty storage. Some covers were missing and of other books there was only the cover – but even a cover can sometimes tell a story. One ragged cloth cover was stitched to a book with Bill's name on it and was dated 1907. On another book was my father's beautiful copperplate writing. That generation took great pride in the art of handwriting, or 'having a good hand' as my grandmother termed it.

Back in those days the books on the curriculum were seldom changed as books cost money and that was a scarce commodity, so schoolbooks were passed down from one family member to another, one generation to another, and indeed often from neighbour to neighbour. So these books had the names of many members of the family and sometimes of old neighbours inscribed in them. When leafing through many of them, I felt like saying: 'Well done, thou good and faithful servant', because these books had indeed taken good care of their contents and served us well.

These were the books that were used in the National Schools of Ireland during the 1940s and 1950s, and probably since independence in the 1920s. Amongst my collection too were copies of books that were used in the early years of the small secondary schools set up around rural Ireland by enterprising young graduates who wished to bring education back to their own place. At that time not every family could afford to send their children to boarding school and in remote rural areas there were no convents and monasteries with nuns and brothers who were then the main educators in cities and towns. Those small rural secondary schools provided second-level education for many of us who would otherwise have gone without. These young educational entrepreneurs could have found jobs in well-established convents or colleges, or emigrated to exciting new places, but chose instead to face an uncertain future and invest their time and money in renting premises to set up these small schools. Sometimes they were following a family tradition – the grandfather of the young man who started our secondary school had, years previously, taught in our old school across the fields. They occasionally provided education for children whose parents were not able to come up with the small fees that they charged. These teachers are the unsung educators and enlighteners of many young minds around rural Ireland. We owe them a debt of gratitude.

Then I came across a wonderful book, *The Secret Life of Books*, by Tom Mole, which made me think about how precious books are. It was another incentive to rescue the old books in the attic. What secrets would they reveal? How would I relate to them now, so many years later? Would they still live or would they have faded from my mind? And so, after long years of wondering quite what to do with these old schoolbooks, a seed was planted and *Books from the Attic* began to take shape. My mother, Gabriel and Con had entrusted the books to me. They should not be lost; their stories and poems are from another time and another place and are a huge part of our culture. So please find a comfortable chair and put your feet up. It's time for the Gobán Saor!

Chapter 2

My New Book

My arrival into first class and being presented with a brand new Kincora Reader was a day to remember. It had a gorgeous smell and you got a thrill of excitement just running your fingers up and down the shiny pages. A brand new *anything* was much appreciated in our world back then!

Our schoolbooks were seldom new. They were 'hand-me-downs', going through large families, and, for me, being sixth in the line of succession, mine always had the evidence of much wear and tear before they eventually reached me. This system of handing on books worked because there was never a change of books on the curriculum. So the acquisition of a pristine, untainted copy was a big occasion. Such a thing would only come about when an old copy of a particular book had absolutely fallen asunder or gone missing. A rare event! We were cautioned to take good care of our books, and we did as we were told because we were well aware that if a precious book went missing there would be '*míle* murder'. Books cost money, and money was hard-earned. So a brand new book was a rare treat. To me it felt almost as if this special book had a life of its own and could almost teach me by itself! The fact that the first lesson in the new book gave instructions on how it should be treated came as no surprise at all – that this new book was actually talking to me was quite within the realm of possibilities. Things could not get any better than that! Each word was absorbed and all the commands that this new book issued were carried out with absolute delight.

Take Care of Me

I am your new book, and I want you to take good care of me. Keep me clean, please, and cover me with stout brown paper. I do not want to look old and torn before my time.

One little person in the front desk – a little person with curly hair – is saying now:

'Books can't talk!'

But this little person is wrong. I *can* talk, for I shall be telling you stories from now until the end of the year. So no one can blame me for saying a little about myself.

You will find a few hard words here and there in my pages. I am sorry about this but it is not my fault.

By the end of the year, too, you will find that these hard words are not so hard as they look. Then you will pass into another class and begin another book.

I hope that I shall be good friends with all of you long before then – even with the curly little person in the front desk.

And now, just before I stop talking about myself, I want you to look once again at the words which stand at the top of this lesson. Take care of me, please, and cover me with brown paper. I do not want to look old and torn before my time.

Every instruction of that lesson was taken in with wide-eyed wonder and on arriving home that evening with my shiny new book, the job of covering this treasure and all our other books was a major undertaking of primary importance. Because all the other books, which may have been in use for years, were still new to whoever was to use them this coming year, they too had to get a fresh new coat.

The choice of outfit was limited. Usually the first choice was brown paper, which had to be carefully cut into shape with scissors. These scissors, though not my mother's best, which were kept in her sewing machine for dress-making, came with a health warning and firm instructions: 'Mind your fingers;' 'Don't stick that scissors into your eye;' 'Don't cut the cover of the book.' If you failed to follow these orders properly, the scissors were smartly whipped off you by an older sister who deemed herself more capable of fulfilling the requirements. Sometimes a battle for supremacy took place which brought another sister on board and a power struggle ensued with no possible solution in sight until a peace treaty was negotiated by my

mother, who constantly poured oil on troubled relationships in our female-dominated household.

The brown paper had arrived during the year wrapped
around messages from town and had been carefully saved
by my mother with this very purpose in mind. Sometimes
paper bags containing meal for the animals or chicken feed
were taken apart, cut up and reused. This slightly crumpled
paper had to be laid out on the table and the wrinkles
eased out with the palms of our hands, or, if the paper
was in a very wrinkled condition, the iron was brought
into action. The iron at the time was a lethal contraption
with an inner space that was entered through a back door
with a smaller iron, which had been previously thrust into
the fire where it remained until glowing red. Then it was
picked out with a long, iron tongs and eased carefully into
the back of the iron. One false move would have dire con-
sequences. When ironing clothes, the hotter the little 'red
divil' was the better, but with brown paper a lesser degree
of heat was required, otherwise the precious brown paper
would crumple and singe into a shadow of its former self.
If this disaster struck, the leading general of the book-cov-
ering squad was quickly swept from power and a more
capable pair of hands put in charge.

The aim was to cover four books from a standard sheet
of brown paper – of course that depended on the size of
the books to be covered. The sheet of paper was spread out
on the kitchen table and four books laid out on top of it. It
took a lot of juggling around with different-sized books to

get the most coverage from one sheet of paper. It was highly desirable to allow sufficient paper for a deep overlap to go inside the cover. If the overlap was too skimpy, the book could slip out of its jacket. This was the era before sellotape came to solve that problem.

If the parlour or one of the bedrooms had been wallpapered earlier in the year, your book could finish up with a matching coat of the same wallpaper. And sometimes we resorted to using other available jackets for our schoolbooks. Testament of our resourcefulness is evident today in my box of books because now, many years later, one of them is still wearing a coat proclaiming Lemon's Pure Sweets; Lemon's was a Dublin sweet company of the time. This box must have come from the local shop and been taken apart because it was sufficiently pliable to be moulded into a jacket for a schoolbook. As a last resort, the *Cork Examiner* newspaper was sometimes brought into action.

When they were covered, we put our books in their new jackets on a chair and sat on them to flatten them into their new attire and mould a better fit. Later that night, when adults gathered around the fire, the books that were not completely flattened were placed beneath bigger, heavier bottoms to mould a total union between book and cover. A well-flattened, firmly-covered book fitted neatly into our school sacks, as we called our schoolbags, but more important still, it was better able to survive the ordeals of the year ahead. And, as well as that, when your books were all kitted out in matching covers there was something

deeply satisfying in standing back to admire your neat stack of books. These firm, new jackets kept the books safe in our school sacks as they journeyed on wet and windy days, going back and forth across fields and over ditches. And on some occasions sacks could be abandoned when more interesting pursuits distracted us, and they might be forgotten on muddy ditches where they could be left to soak in heavy showers of rain. So our schoolbooks had to be well buttoned up to cope with all kinds of weather eventualities.

My new book got me off to a flying start: two of the poems caught my attention immediately as they were about a subject very close to my heart – the fairies.

Chapter 3

Fairyland

Growing up in an Ireland where fairyland was part of the landscape added an extra dimension to life, especially for us children for whom nothing was outside the realm of possibility. In our world, fairies were capable of doing anything. The fact that a leprechaun (lepracaun) or 'elf man', could lead you to a pot of gold at the end of the rainbow was an amazing opportunity to be grasped if the chance ever came your way. Catching a leprechaun would be like winning the Lotto in today's world, and you could never rule out the possibility that it just might happen. So a poem about him in my new book was very exciting.

The Fairy Shoemaker

I caught him at work one day, myself,
In the castle-ditch, where foxglove grows –
A wrinkled, wizened, and bearded elf,
Spectacles stuck on his pointed nose,
Silver buckles on his hose.

The rogue was mine, beyond a doubt,
I stared at him; he stared at me;
'Servant, Sir!' 'Humph!' says he,
And pulled a snuff-box out.
He took a long pinch, looked better pleased,
The queer little Lepracaun;
Offered the box with a whimsical grace –
Pouf! he flung the dust in my face,
And, while I sneezed,
Was gone!

William Allingham

Just beside our farmhouse, as in many other farms around the country, was an old fort and we grew up with an awareness of this historic place, which was a series of rings around which my father had planted trees beneath which we constantly played. My father had historical explanations for the origins of this fort, but we much preferred our old neighbour Mrs Casey's stories about the fairies or the 'little people' who lived there. To us these unseen people were as real as the farm animals and our constant dream was to take one of them by surprise and have a chat with them. So when poems and stories about fairies appeared in our schoolbooks it made that possibility seem more attainable.

The poems and stories in our books confirmed our belief that the elf man was not very friendly, though we knew there were good fairies and bad fairies. We were a little bit in awe of them all, and a little scared of the elf man. The fact that in my new schoolbook someone had actually taken a little elf man by surprise and had chatted with him was fantastic. Maybe we too could do that!

The Little Elf Man
I saw a little elf man once,
Down where the lilies blow.
I asked him why he was so small,
And why he didn't grow.

He slightly frowned, and with his eye
He looked me through and through.
'I'm quite as big for me,' said he,
'As you are big for you.'

John K. Bangs

This poem was illustrated with a black-and-white drawing of an elf and a little girl, which I decided had to be me. And, unfortunately, despite all the instructions about taking good care of this new book, I made efforts to improve on the illustrator with red crayon!

Mrs Casey had an implicit belief in another world peopled by beings of whom we had no understanding. This was the era of home births, and she helped the local midwife bring each one of us into the world. On one such occasion on his way into town to collect Nurse Burke, the midwife, my father as usual alerted Mrs Casey to the forthcoming event. She lit a candle and proceeded down the boreen from her cottage to our house bearing the candle aloft, and on arrival told my mother, 'They came with me when I had the blessed candle.' 'They' could either be the souls of departed Taylors or the little people from the fort, as all were encompassed in her world. I always think of her when someone quotes these lines from *Hamlet*:

There are more things in heaven and earth, Horatio,
Than are dreamt of in your philosophy.

She constantly told us that the little people helped us to do some of our farm work – an announcement at which my father smiled in amusement, but still, he never interfered with the land in and around the fort and fenced it off so that the farm animals did not have access to it. Many farmers who had old forts on their land followed this practice and thus preserved these historic places which are part of our heritage. Also, tales abounded of the bad luck that came the way of families who interfered with these places, so the people of the time had great respect for that unknown world. But for us children this world gave rein to our imagination and when we played in the fort we felt sure that around us was another hidden world, and even though we could not see them the fairies were keeping a wary eye on us. So when we learned poems in school confirming the magic abilities of the fairy people, we were delighted.

A New Year Call
A fairy came to call me
At twilight time to-day.
He coasted down an icicle,
But said he couldn't stay
For more that sixty-seven blinks
To Happy-New-Year me;
And wouldn't take his mittens off
For he had had his tea.

He sat upon the window-sill,
His wings all puckered in,
And talked about the New Year deeds
He thought he would begin;
He said he'd help the fairies more
And bird and flower folk;
He'd teach the kittens how to purr
And baby frogs to croak.

This year, he said, he'd practise up
His fairy scales and sing
The woodland world all wide awake

By twenty winks to Spring;
He'd never tease the butterflies,
Nor mock the whip-poor-wills,
But he would feed the daisies dew
And dust the daffodils.

And he would mind his fairy queen
For years and years and years,
And wear his rubbers when he should
And wash behind his ears.
He perked his wings up then, and winked
And sang a good-bye tune,
Then left a snowflake calling-card
And flew up to the moon.

Marjorie Barrows

Another poem about the fairies rolled off our tongues and had the added bonus that as you recited it you could do an accompanying little dance. We pranced around the kitchen table pretending to be fairies as we recited it until we knew every word.

The Fairies
Up the airy mountain
Down the rushy glen,
We daren't go a-hunting
For fear of little men;
Wee folk, good folk

Trooping all together
Green jacket, red cap,
And white owl's feather.

Down along the rocky shore
Some make their home–
They live on crispy pancakes
Of yellow tide-foam;
Some in the reeds
Of the black mountain lake,
With frogs for their watch-dogs,
All night awake.

By the craggy hill-side,
Through the mosses bare
They have planted thorn trees
For pleasure here and there.
Is any man so daring
As dig one up in spite,
He shall find their sharpest thorns
In his bed at night.

Up the airy mountain,
Down the rushy glen,
We daren't go a-hunting
For fear of little men;
Wee folk, good folk,
Trooping all together

> Green jacket, red cap,
> And white owl's feather.

William Allingham

As we learned this poem we could visualise the fairies running up and down the hilly field beside our fort and the fact that we also had a rushy glen further up the valley from the Fort Field completed this imaginary picture.

To confirm our belief in the fairies, or the little people, there were also stories, as well as poems, in our schoolbooks about them. Who could doubt what Mrs. Ryan saw with her own two eyes?

Mrs. Ryan and the Little Man

It was ten o'clock. The October evenings were chilly, but Mrs. Ryan's kitchen was a warm and pleasant place to be in. She sat spinning by the fire, and should have been very happy.

But the wool kept tangling and knotting. Once or twice she was almost sure she heard somebody or something pattering across the floor. She felt that somebody was peeping round a corner at her, saying 'Hurry up! Hurry up! Hurry up!'

She put away her spinning-wheel and went upstairs to bed, very uneasy, for it was the third night this had happened.

'There is something very queer about the house,' she said, 'and the sooner I find what it is the better.'

Next morning she set off to see the Wise Woman, who lived across the valley. She asked her advice.

'The evenings are getting cold and frosty, Mrs. Ryan,' said

the Wise Woman, 'and you are not the only one that likes a
warm hearth. You had better leave the kitchen to the one that
wants it. Go up to bed at nine o'clock to-night. But before
you go to bed, sit on the top step of the stairs and watch a bit.
You'll see what you'll see.'

That night Mrs. Ryan went upstairs at nine o'clock, and sat
on the top step to watch.

There was a rustling from the donkey's shed next the
kitchen. Through a chink in the wall came a head – the head
of a little old man with a long white beard and a pointed red
cap. He looked all around the room to make sure that there
was no one there but the cats. Then he squeezed through the
chink and jumped down. He turned head over heels three
times, and lit cross-legged on the warm hearthstone right
between the two cats. They seemed to know him.

Out of one pocket he took a tiny hammer and some tiny
nails. Out of another he took the smallest shoe of red leather
you ever saw. And he began to hammer away at the heel of
the shoe – tack–tack–tack–a–tack–tack. As he hammered, he
sang to himself like a little cricket on the hearth.

'So that's who it was,' said Mrs. Ryan, 'pattering about,
trying to get to the fire. The creature, the poor cold little
creature! He shall have the hearth to himself, and welcome,
for the rest of the winter.'

Each winter night after that Mrs. Ryan went to bed at
nine o'clock and left her kitchen to the little man. She had
an hour less for spinning, but she got as much done, for the
wheel went fast and smoothly, the thread never broke nor
tangled, and the yarn was always even and soft.

Another poem, with the magical tile of 'The Fairy Tree',
which was also a song, really came alive when at Christmas
my father brought home a record with the famous tenor
John McCormack singing it. We played the record again
and again on the gramophone until we had learnt the
words and could sing it along with him. The fact that the
fairies who lived in our fort were also on our gramophone
records as well as in our schoolbooks cemented our belief
in them. One wonders if they were the Harry Potter of
our time, fanning children's imaginations about the world
of fantasy.

The Fairy Tree
All night around the thorn tree
The little people play,
And men and women passing
Will turn their heads away.
From break of dawn til moonrise,
Alone it stands on high,
With twisted sprigs for branches
Across the winter sky.

They'll tell you dead men hung there,
Its black and bitter fruit,
To guard the buried treasure
Round which it twines its root.
They'll tell you Cromwell hung them,
But that could never be,

He'd be in dread like others
To touch the Fairy Tree.

But Katie Ryan who saw there
In some sweet dream she had,
The Blessed Son of Mary
And all His face was sad.
She dreamt she heard Him saying:
'Why should they be afraid
When from a branch of thorn tree
The crown I wore was made?'

From moonrise round the thorn tree
The little people play
And men and women passing
Will turn their heads away.
But if your heart's a child's heart
And if your eyes are clean,
You'll never fear the thorn tree
That grows beyond Clogheen.

Isabel Leslie (alias Temple Lane)

In the middle of one of the fields down by the river that
ran along the bottom of our farm was a blackthorn tree. In
winter its black twisted branches arched against the sky with
a menacing appearance, but in spring, when it burst into
white blossom, it transformed itself into a blaze of white
wonder. To us it had to be a Fairy Tree. These trees have

often defied the laws of legal logic and even caused roads to circumvent them in order not to disturb the mythical lore surrounding them.

Growing up in a world where money was a scarce commodity it was easy to envy the fairies for whom money seemed to be of no consequence at all.

The Fairies

The fairies have never a penny to spend,
They haven't a thing put by,
But theirs is the dower of bird and flower
And theirs is the earth and sky.
And though you should live in a palace of gold
Or sleep in a dried-up ditch,
You could never be poor as the fairies are,
And never as rich.

Since ever and ever the world began
They have danced like a ribbon of flame,
They have sung their song through the centuries long
And yet it is never the same.
And though you be foolish or though you be wise,
With hair of silver or gold
You could never be young as the fairies are,
And never as old.

Rose Fyleman

Chapter 4

No-nonsense Nana

Reclining on her raised pedestal of pillows my grand-mother enshrined her black iron bed in a nightly rosary of benedictions. Having first wound up her weights-and-chains clock and liberally doused the two of us in a shower of holy water, she climbed on board her high, brass-knobbed chariot for the night. When she had settled all the pillows to her satisfaction she began her rosary, which went on and on, and if my voice trailed off into sleep in the middle of a 'Holy Mary', I got a sharp poke in the back to get me back to the job on hand. On completion of the rosary, to which many amendments were added, came the piece I liked best when she summoned the four Evangelists to take up their nightly duty.

Matthew, Mark, Luke and John
Bless this bed that I lie on

And if I die before I wake
My soul I give the Lord to take.
Having put the Evangelists on duty and the Lord on standby, we could rest easy for the night, leaving all emergencies in their capable hands, while we sailed, well-guarded, into the land of nod. It never crossed my grandmother's mind that her instructions could be disobeyed. She never questioned the presence of God, he was all around her house and part of her outside world as well. Our schoolbooks reflected that belief.

I See His Blood upon the Rose
I see his blood upon the rose
And in the stars the glory of his eyes,
His body gleams amid eternal snows
His tears fall from the skies.

I see his face in every flower;
The thunder and the singing of the birds
Are but his voice – and carven by his power
Rocks are his written words.

All pathways by his feet are worn,
His strong heart stirs the ever-beating sea,
His crown of thorns is twined with every thorn
His cross is every tree.

Joseph Mary Plunkett

In this poem the divine, human, and the natural are seamlessly blended into everyday living. That was my grandmother's world. God was on duty above and she was on duty below. On occasions when she might have thought that a little divine guidance was necessary she consulted with him. But on the whole she felt that she was doing a pretty good job and never doubted her ability to sort out eventualities that came her way. This was at a time when bishops were belting people with their croziers, with which she was not impressed, and in this instance she and my father held similar views, which was not always the case. Standing between the two of them was my pacifist mother, a compliant Catholic, whose conversion to their way of thinking was out of the question because no one could argue with my mother, who was one of the 'I'm on my way to heaven and I shall not be moved' brigade.

My grandmother was a political animal and a staunch republican, with which views my father did not agree, so it was a case of 'Don't mention the war.' She was the material of the French Revolution and if the necessity had arisen would have been quite capable of swiping the head off a haughty aristocrat.

She did not suffer fools gladly and put manners on us when we were dispatched back to my mother's original home place, where Nana presided. She loved and took good care of her animals, but when the necessity for survival arose she could efficiently wring the neck of a chicken or a duck, or put a quick stop to the gallop of a pig that was needed for winter sustenance, which was all part of the self-sufficient food chain of the time. She was the only woman in our neighbourhood to kill her own pig, which was a fairly barbaric exercise, but because she was a widow with no mature male butcher in the house she got on with it and did what had to be done. I was slightly scared of her, but also very impressed by her. She blended her kitchen, her fields, her animals and the divine all into the one major mix, which to me was awe-inspiring.

In some way that is beyond understanding or explanation, when I learned the following poem it encompassed my grandmother's world. I remember standing inside the kitchen window on a wet spring evening learning it for school and being stirred by a profound sympathy for the sheep and lambs, but also feeling a deeper sadness beyond my understanding. My grandmother's world was in that poem.

Sheep and Lambs
All in the April evening
April airs are abroad;
The sheep with their little lambs
Passed me by on the road.

The sheep with their little lambs
Passed me by on the road;
All in the April evening
I thought on the Lamb of God.

The lambs were weary and crying
With a weak, human cry.
I thought on the Lamb of God
Going meekly to die.

Up in the blue, blue mountains
Dewy pastures are sweet;
Rest for the little bodies,
Rest for the little feet.

But for the Lamb of God
Up on the hill-top green
Only a cross of shame
Two stark crosses between.

All in the April evening,
April airs were abroad;
I saw the sheep with their lambs
And thought on the Lamb of God.

Katharine Tynan

Interwoven though the pages of our schoolbooks were lessons about the natural world and how it balanced and protected us, the animals and itself. My grandmother was part of that world and, like the hedgehog in the following story, she was admirable though not very cuddlesome!

The Hedgehog

As soon as the hedgehog is a few weeks old he has to make his own bed, for his mother pays no more attention to him. He creeps under a bush in the wood, scratches a little hole, and lies down in it. When he lies down he rolls himself up into a little ball, with his head and his tail tucked into his paws, and his prickly bristles standing up all round him. No one who finds him can touch him without being pricked. Even a dog will stand and bark at him but will not dare to bite him.

All day long the hedgehog lies still in his little room, but when evening comes he wakes up and stretches himself, for to him this is the break of day, and the moon will give him light. He lays back his prickles, stretches out his snout and follows the lead of his nose.

His eyesight is bad, but his sense of smell is very keen. Should you meet him and stand quite still in his path, he may run right up without noticing you, but if his nose touches your shoe, he instantly rolls himself up in a prickly ball. He will stay rolled up for some time before he stretches himself out again and trots off.

It is during the night that the hedgehog hunts for food. He picks up the cockchafer crawling on the ground, or swallows the worm that comes up from under the soil to taste the evening dew. When he comes to a mouse-hole he sniffs around to find out if Miss Mouse is at home or out for a walk. He scents the exact spot where she is hidden and begins to tear up the earth with his snout. The little mouse is so terrified that she forgets to run away and the hedgehog soon catches her and eats her up.

In field and forest the hedgehog does much useful work. Farmers spare his life and often take him home to catch mice in their stables and barns. As soon as cockroaches and crickets come out of their crannies and chinks the hedgehog pounces on them and eats them up. If you keep a hedgehog in your house you must give him a little bread and milk every day.

When autumn comes and the leaves fall from the trees, the hedgehog begins to think of making up his bed for the winter. He scratches his little bedroom deeper into the ground and collects a whole heap of leaves, straw, and grass. Where the wind has blown the leaves together into a pile he rolls round and round, till his prickles are covered with them. He then looks like a heap of moving foliage. With these he trots home, strips off each leaf, and then goes off again to fetch straw from the stubble field. From the outside his house does not look tidy, but inside it the hedgehog twists himself round and round till he has made for himself a neat round room. Here he curls up when the weather gets very cold, and goes to sleep. There is no food for him then in field or forest. The beetles are dead, the worms have crept deep down into the ground, and even the mice will not dare to come out from the holes below the frozen soil.

Every beast knows how to tide over the evil days of winter; the song-birds fly to warmer countries, the squirrels live on their winter store of nuts, but the hedgehog sleeps the winter through on his little bed of leaves. What does for one will not do for another.

R. Wagner

Hedgehogs were part of our childhood, but a sighting is now quite rare. A few years ago I had a Doberman called Kate who was always on the prowl, sniffing around under the hedges in the garden. One night she came into the kitchen with what I thought was a scrubbing brush in her mouth. But when I investigated I discovered a hedgehog between her jaws. I was dubious about returning it to my own garden lest there was a repeat performance, so I carried it to a neighbour who had no dogs. We were a bit worried that Kate had done lethal damage, but not so, because the following day the hedgehog had moved on. Extricating a hedgehog from the jaws of a Doberman was not an easy process, but I think my grandmother would have approved.

Chapter 5

Inside the Farm Gate

Our food came from the fields all around us. The spring planting led to the autumn harvest and then the grain went to the mill and came back as brown and white flour that became our daily bread. Our meat came from the pigs rooting in the haggard, and the chickens, ducks and geese wandering around the farmyard. Hen eggs were in constant supply. Potatoes and vegetables dug up in the morning were on the table for our midday dinner. The milk from the morning milking was in use soon afterwards and indeed we often sampled it while still warm from the cows. During winter months, when milk intake reduced, removing the need for the daily journey to the creamery, we made our own butter. The making of butter necessitated separating the skim milk from the cream, which after a few days resting, was churned into butter. However, before the cream

found its way into the churn some of it could be diverted into cream jugs to be poured over porridge and desserts. My sister Ellen adored cream and was quite capable of downing a cup with glee when my mother was not looking. The cats too loved any cream that they could get at; that's probably where the phrase 'the cat who got the cream', indicating self-satisfaction, originated.

We had never heard of foraging, but we were foragers! As we rambled through fields and over ditches we helped ourselves to haws, sloes, nuts, blackberries, wild raspberries, and gathered cup-mushrooms to bring home and bake on hot sods of turf by the fire. We knew the lie of the land and where to source the cup mushrooms – these were the ideal receptacle to hold a flow of salt which sizzled into a gorgeous-tasting liquid within the mushroom, which added greatly to the flavour of the final feast. The hazel trees on the ditch of the Fort field were eagerly climbed at Halloween to provide a supply of nuts that were collected in tin gallons as we clung to the highest branches to reach those dangling in bunches almost out of reach. Sometimes we overreached ourselves and hung on for dear life until the branch cracked and we hit the ground with a hard thump, which enlisted very little sympathy from our fellow climbers. But there was a skill in ascertaining which nuts were mature enough to gain entry into our gallons. Some under-ripe ones were easily recognised by their green stems, but others had to be tested by tooth to check whether they were sufficiently mature to make the grade. Our quality-control procedure consisted of sight, touch and taste.

When the gallons were full we bore them home in the gathering dusk, but sometimes on the way home we had a hair-raising encounter when Mick, who worked with us on the farm, and my brother, who was the eldest, decided to play ghosts and ghouls, wrapped themselves in white sheets and sent out blood-curdling banshee noises from the fort. Though we knew quite well who it was, we still ran home yelling and screaming in delicious fright, much to the annoyance of my father who was not into such foolish carry-on. Once safely home the gallons of nuts were up-ended to be cracked open on the flagstone in front of the fire.

At Halloween, the old apple trees in the orchard below the house provided the needful for the 'snap apple' challenge when we hung a large apple by a string from a hook in the ceiling. Already in place along the ceiling were two rows of hooks used to hang the bacon for curing and before the decision was made about exactly on which hook the apple was to be hung there was usually a big argument as to which hook was deemed the most central as plenty of floor space beneath was necessary for the mobility of the apple catcher. When we could not reach a unanimous agreement, my father, who was the apple hanger, stepped in and took a ministerial decision. No one argued with that. Then we took our turns at grabbing the apple with open jaws as it spun around in midair. There was a lot of arguing about length-of-time entitlements, but eventually, when each of us had had our turn and that source of entertainment was exhausted we began the more splashy operation of catching with our mouths an apple floating in a large white enamel pan full of water in the centre of the kitchen table. Here, as the apple swam around in the water, each one of us in turn became sharks in pursuit. This resulted in water spraying in all directions and arguments over the lack of observation of impromptu rules – and eventually, when we were all like drowned rats and the kitchen in a sorry state, my mother called a halt and began to make cocoa, which was the usual nighttime beverage. We were dispatched upstairs to return in our nightdresses and gather around the fire, where Bill told us ghost stories, which were all part of Halloween. Later, going upstairs to bed, we checked to make sure that none of Bill's ghosts or ghouls was hiding under the beds or behind the doors.

The river that ran along the valley at the bottom of the land was also a source of sustenance. Every Sunday afternoon throughout summer my father went fishing and brought home a bagful of gleaming, slithering trout. The fresh trout roasted in butter by my mother in the bastable over the fire were gorgeous, but prior to that they had to be gutted and cleaned in the spout at the end of the yard. This was our job, one which we did not savour very much, and sometimes we wished that the catch was less, ungrateful brats that we were! Sometimes, after a day out shooting, a pheasant, woodcock, grouse or snipe was landed on the table. My grandmother advocated snipe soup in the treatment of TB, which was the 'virus' of the time.

On a very rare occasion a hare came our way and that was an extra special treat – which probably led to the legendary Mrs Beeton advising in her recipe for hare soup: 'First catch your hare.' This was no easy task. The sighting of a hare was rare and it was a thrill even to catch a quick glimpse of one. There is something almost mythical about the hare. Sleek and elegant, they are always on high alert for intruders and bound away instantly on long sleek legs at the first sight of humans. Sometimes they can be heard pounding the earth with their hind legs as if they are sending out a red-alert signal to fellow hares. A very, very rare and wonderful sight is to see two of them facing each other and take each other on, both up on their hind legs, and it is difficult to know then if they are dancing together or challenging each other.

My grandmother had huge appreciation of any game or wild fowl that were brought to her kitchen door and she had a special ritual for their cooking. She set great store on hare soup and considered it a rare delicacy that was capable of curing strange and undiagnosed ailments. She had a complicated procedure for the cooking of a hare and even as a child I sensed that while this undertaking was being carried out it was best to keep a low profile and your mouth shut in case you upset the delicate balance involved in this specialised culinary undertaking.

Some years ago amongst the books in the attic I found an old, tattered copy of Mrs Beeton's cookery book containing exact, and exacting, instructions on all kinds of household management. It was ragged, without a cover and stained from years of use, so I took it up to Kenny's bookbindery in Galway to have it restored and bound. The section on the preparation of game and fowl for the oven included detailed recipes for cooking hare – Hashed and Jugged. Obviously, Mrs Beeton had caught her hare.

HARE, HASHED

INGREDIENTS. –Remains of cold roast hare, 3/4 pint of brown sauce, I glass of port or claret, salt and pepper, red-currant jelly.

METHOD. –Cut the hare into neat slices, and put these aside while the bones and trimmings are being boiled for stock. Make the brown sauce as directed, and, when economy is an object, use equal parts of stock and stout instead of adding wine to the sauce when finished. Season the sauce to taste, put in the slices of hare, let them remain until thoroughly hot, then serve with red-currant jelly.
TIME –15 minutes, to reheat the hare. AVERAGE COST, 1s. 4d. to Is. 6d.

BROWN SAUCE
INGREDIENTS. –1 pint of brown stock, 2 oz. of butter, 11/2 oz. of flour, 1 small carrot, 1 small onion, 6 fresh button mushrooms (when in season). 1 tomato, salt and pepper.

METHOD. –Slice the mushrooms, carrot, and onion and fry them until brown in the butter. Sprinkle in the flour, stir, and cook for a few minutes, then add the sliced tomato and stock, and stir until it boils. Simmer for 10 minutes, season to taste, strain or pass through a tammy-cloth, re-heat, and serve. Pre-served mushrooms may be used, but they do not impart the same flavour to the sauce. A tablespoonful of good mushroom ketchup is an improvement.

TIME. —40 to 45 minutes. AVERAGE COST, about 6*d*, exclusive of the stock.

It puts one in mind of the TV programme *Lords and Ladles* where we gasp in amazement at the amount of food con-sumed at one of those grand dinners. One would wonder if Mrs Beeton's cookery book might have been in use downstairs, because she was the Myrtle Allen of her time. Undoubtedly, all the ingredients for all those grand feasts in that programme were sourced from inside the castle gate. And though my grandmother did not have a huge castle estate, she still had the high quality of her own farm food.

The hare was elusive and smart, but one of the stories in our schoolbook proved that there was someone out there smarter than the hare. On learning this lesson we were very impressed by the cleverness of the tortoise. Did it teach us that even when the odds were stacked against you, there might still be a solution?

The Hare and the Tortoise

A hare and a tortoise agreed to run a race.

'Where shall we run to?' asked the hare, who was quite sure of winning.

'To the top of the corn-field and back five times,' said the tortoise.

'Right,' said the hare, and away he flew, leaving the tortoise at the starting-post.

Up and down the field went the hare, running as fast as he could, but he could never overtake the tortoise. When he got to the top of the field it was always there in front of him, and each time he came back to the starting point again it was there too.

After the hare had run four lengths of the field, he lost heart, and stopped.

'I am too quick for you,' said the tortoise. 'I beat you easily, although I took a rest now and then.'

The poor hare said nothing, but slunk away with his tail between his legs. He did not know that there were two tortoises in the field, one at the top and one at the bottom, and that neither of them had moved an inch during the race.

At the very beginning of this lesson you felt sorry for the tortoise, but you finished up feeling sorry for the hare.

Unlike the hares, the fields were strewn with rabbits who scampered off in all directions when we climbed over a ditch or ran through a gap and took them by surprise. While the hare was practically invisible, the rabbits were happy and free, hopping around with their white tails bobbing, and the baby ones were little balls of fur on four scampering legs. At the time there was a big market for rabbits for food and so sometimes the poor rabbits finished up as victims of snaring, which resulted in this very sad poem that we learned in school.

The Snare

I hear a sudden cry of pain!
There is a rabbit in a snare:
Now I hear the cry again,
But I cannot tell from where.

But I cannot tell from where
He is calling out for aid,
Crying on the frightened air,
Making everything afraid.

Making everything afraid.
Wrinkling up his little face,
As he cries again for aid;
And I cannot find the place!

And I cannot find the place
Where his paw is in the snare:
Little One! Oh, Little One!
I am searching everywhere.

James Stephens

Chapter 6

On the Wing

Growing up in the depths of the country, the bird world was part of our world and blended seamlessly into our thinking. That some of the poems we learned in school were about birds was an additional plus as it all danced together. We watched the swallows come every spring and sweep in flocks into the barns, stables and cow houses, where they moved back into their old rooftop dwellings along the rafters. Their coming marked the beginning of summer. We had a lot in common with the birds in the following poem that I remember well.

Bird Thoughts
I lived once in a little house,
And lived there very well;

I thought the world was small and round,
And made of pale blue shell.

I lived next in a little nest,
Nor needed any other;
I thought the world was made of straw,
And builded by my mother.

The day I flew down from the nest
To see what I could find.
'The world is made of leaves,' I said,
'I have been very blind.'

And then I flew beyond the tree,
Quite fit for grown-up labours;
'I don't know how the world is made
And neither do my neighbours.'

Coming home from school we looked out for and inspected birds' nests along the way. When peering into their feathery nests we held our breaths as we believed that the mother bird, on coming home, would get a whiff of an intruder from our breathing and abandon the nest. That would be a disaster as far as we were concerned. So we were very careful to leave no trace, but were totally fascinated by birds' nests all the same. The following poem could have been written for us.

Birds' Nests

The skylark's nest among the grass
And waving corn is found;
The robin's on a shady bank,
With oak leaves strewn around.

The wren builds in an ivied thorn,
Or old and ruined wall;
The mossy nest, so covered in,
You scarce can see at all.

The martins build their nests of clay,
In rows beneath the eaves;
While silvery lichens, moss and hair,
The chaffinch interweaves.

The cuckoo makes no nest at all,
But through the wood she strays
Until she finds one snug and warm,
And there her egg she lays.

The sparrow has a nest of hay,
With feathers warmly lined;
The ring-dove's careless nest of sticks
On lofty trees we find.

Rooks build together in a wood,
And often disagree;

The owl will build inside a barn
Or in a hollow tree.

The blackbird's nest of grass and mud
In brush and bank is found;
The lapwing's darkly spotted eggs
Are laid upon the ground.

The magpie's nest is girt with thorns
in leafless trees or hedge;
The wild duck and water-hen
Build by the water's edge.

Birds build their nests from year to year,
According to their kind,
Some very neat and beautiful
Some easily designed.

The habits of each little bird,
And all its patient skill,
Are surely taught by God Himself
And ordered by His will.

Anonymous

The water hens in the river were another source of delight
for us as we meandered home from school. We hung in over
the small stone bridge to watch them float along and disappear into the overflowing greenery along the banks. We

were very impressed with the long-legged 'Joany the Bogs', who could stand forever on one leg surveying all around her. The wonders of the bird world were many. But maybe the first call of the cuckoo was the most exciting thing of all. We listened out to hear that sound and our delight on hearing her was not lessened by her bad habit of usurping the rights of smaller birds in the nest. It was an extension to our world to discover that there were poems and lessons about the cuckoo in our schoolbooks.

Cuckoo
His voice runs before me; I follow, it flies;
It is now in the meadow, and now 'mid the skies;
So blithesome, so lightsome, now distant, now here,
And when he calls Cuckoo, the summer is near.

He calls back the roses, red roses that went
At the first blast of winter, so sad and forspent,
With the dew in their bosoms, young roses and dear,
And when he calls Cuckoo, the summer is near.

I would twine him a gold cage, but what would he do
For his world of the emerald, his bath in the blue,
And his wee feathered comrades to make him good
    cheer?
And when he calls Cuckoo, the summer is near.

Now, blackbird, give over your harping of gold!
Brown thrush and green linnet, your music withhold!
The flutes of the forest are silver and clear,
But when he calls Cuckoo, the summer is here.

Katharine Tynan

And we had our own little verse that we chanted as we waited to hear the cuckoo call. He and the corncrake were the voices of our summer. During the day we cooed back to the cuckoo on the off-chance that he might answer us, and at night we went to sleep to the sound of the corncrake as he 'craked' late into the night in the grove below the house. We had a little verse for each of them:

Corncrake out late

Ate mate on Friday morning.

At that time it was a big offence to eat meat on Friday, though I doubt that the corncrake was aware of Church laws and regulations. As we waited for the cuckoo and when he arrived, we serenaded him with this little chant:

The cuckoo comes in April

Sings his song in May

In the middle of June

He plays his tune

And July he flies away.

We absolutely loved the call of the cuckoo and often ran through the field trying to find his location, but as Katharine Tynan's poem describes, he was very elusive and always somewhere else. But there was another side to the cuckoo with which it was hard to be sympathetic. We knew this story well and when a row evolved between us we could accuse each other of being like 'a cuckoo in the nest.'

The Cuckoo in the Nest

The cuckoo does not return to Ireland until the end of April. She comes when the buds are opening on the trees, and the banks are thick with primroses. Birds which have nests to build come much earlier than this, but the cuckoo takes her time.

The cuckoo does not build a nest of her own, but makes use of the nests of other birds – robins, hedge-sparrows and wag-tails. When she finds a nest she takes one of the eggs from it, and puts one of her own in its place. The owners of the nest hatch the cuckoo's egg with the rest, and never seem to know that a trick has been played upon them.

The young cuckoo, when it breaks from the shell, is a very ugly fellow indeed, and it fidgets all the time. There is a tender spot on its back, and it cannot bear to have anything touch it. It twists and shoves, until the other young birds are pushed in turn to the edge of the nest, and fall to the ground.

A few tiny squeaks come from them, and then there is silence, for they soon die of cold and hunger. The cuckoo does not mind, and, strange to say, the parents do not seem to mind either. They are as proud as peacocks of their fine baby.

Very soon the young cuckoo is far bigger than the parent birds, who have to work very hard gathering food for it. They feed it with slugs and insects until it swells like a balloon. At last when it is even too big for the nest, it flaps its wings and flies off. The poor, tired parent birds fly with it, and still

nest, when it is ... , it flaps its wings ... tired parent birds ... keep it supplied with ... till they bring it, and ... ugh, ... feed the young ... see a young ... -sparrows, ... dd tit-bit ... agtails. ... ble to ... nd ... g

MY SHADOW.

I HAVE a little shadow that goes in and out
  with me,
And what can be the use of him is more
  than I can see.
He is very, very like me, from the heels
  up to the head;
I see him jump before me, when I
  jump into my bed.

est thing about him is the way
  to grow—
e proper children, which is
  slow;

keep it supplied with food. It gobbles up all they bring it, and never seems to have enough.

Other birds then help to feed the young giant. So you may sometimes see a young cuckoo being fed by the hedge-sparrows who reared it, and getting an odd tit-bit between meals from robins and wagtails.

After a few weeks the cuckoo is able to seek out its own food. It flies here and there during the summer months, getting stronger and stronger every day. When September comes it rises up into the air and sets off on its long flight to the warm south.

It was hard to swallow the selfishness of the cuckoo and to discover that this bird, whom we loved to hear, was capable of such cruelty to little baby birds. But it introduced us at an early age to the fact that nature follows the rule of 'tooth and claw'. This was a sobering realisation, but we were glad to learn from our schoolbooks that many birds had a more loving approach to life.

What the Birds Say
Do you ask what the birds say? The sparrow, the dove,
The linnet and thrush say, 'I love and I love!'
In winter they're silent – the wind is so strong,
What it says, I don't know, but it sings a loud song.
But green leaves and blossoms and sunny warm
    weather
And singing and loving – all come back together.
But the lark is so brimful of gladness and love,

The green fields below him, the blue sky above,
That he sings, and he sings, and for ever sings he—
'I love my Love, and my Love loves me!'

S. T. Coleridge

But, of all the birds, the robin was the one that we children knew and loved best. He was lovably cheeky and when the kitchen door was wide open in summer he hopped in to see what was going on inside. My mother, though, was a bit wary of him as an old superstition held that he brought news of a forthcoming death. But to us he was a thing of joy, and poems about him were an added delight. The following is probably the one we all remember best.

Robin Redbreast
Good-bye, good-bye to Summer!
For Summer's nearly done;
The garden smiling faintly,
Cool breezes in the sun;
Our thrushes now are silent,
Our swallows flown away –
But Robin's here in coat of brown
With ruddy breast-knot gay.
Robin, Robin Redbreast,
O Robin dear!
Robin sings so sweetly
In the falling of the year.

Bright yellow, red and orange
The leaves come down in hosts;
The trees are Indian princes,
But soon they'll turn to ghosts;
The leathery pears and apples
Hang russet on the bough;
It's Autumn, Autumn, Autumn late,
'Twill soon be winter now.
Robin, Robin Redbreast,
O Robin dear!
And what will this poor Robin do?
For pinching days are near.

The fireside for the cricket,
The wheatstack for the mouse,
When trembling night-winds whistle
And moan all round the house.
The frosty ways like iron,
The branches plumed with snow –
Alas! in winter dead and dark,
Where can poor Robin go?
Robin, Robin Redbreast,
O Robin dear!
And a crumb of bread for Robin
His little heart to cheer.

William Allingham

The robin is the bird for all seasons. As soon as you go into the garden and drive a spade into the earth, the robin immediately arrives to investigate what treasures you might unearth to tempt his palate. He knows no fear and will almost hop on top of your spade. His friendly presence brightens up the bleakest day. But it is during the snow that he really comes into his own with his bright plumage contrasting vividly with the pristine white surroundings. When I was a child there was no such thing as bird feeders, nor any need for them because the birds descended in flocks when the hens and other farm fowl and animals were fed. When the pigs had messily slugged off the contents of their iron troughs and lay contentedly prone on the ground around them, the birds swooped down, making a landing strip of the impervious pigs, and pecked the troughs clean beside them. The cornfields and meadows were food havens and safe nesting places for the wildlife and often when walking through those fields we caught thrilling glimpses of startled hares or caused feeding pheasants to take flight. But things changed when winter came and the fields were bare of food, so we would sprinkle breadcrumbs on the snow and then run back into the kitchen and sit inside the window waiting with great anticipation for the birds to swoop down and begin to eat. We were delighted with all of them, but the robin was our favourite. We loved him.

The Robin

When all the ground with snow is white,
The merry robin comes,
And hops about with great delight
To find the scattered crumbs.

How glad he seems when he can get
A piece of cake or bread!
He has no shoes upon his feet,
Nor hat upon his head.

But happiest is he, I know,
Because no cage with bars
Keeps him from walking in the snow
And printing it with stars.

Frank Dempster Sherman

We had great sympathy with the birds in winter because we could really identify with them, and indeed many other poems in our schoolbooks were akin to our way of living too. The following poem was especially real to us because with no heating in our house, this is exactly what we did to keep warm — it was not unusual for us to have hunts around the kitchen table, and skipping was a regular contest to see who could keep going the longest. So, in order to keep warm we kept moving!

The North Wind Doth Blow

The north wind doth blow, and we shall have snow,
And what will the robin do then, poor thing?
He'll sit in the barn, and keep himself warm
And hide his head under his wing, poor thing!

The north wind doth blow, and we shall have snow
And what will the swallow do then, poor thing?
Oh, do you not know he's gone long ago
To a land that is warmer than ours, poor thing.

The north wind doth blow, and we shall have snow,
And what will the children do then, poor things?
When lessons are done, they'll jump, skip and run,
And play till they keep themselves warm, poor things.

Anonymous

There was another poem in our Kincora Reader about the death of a robin with which we identified. On the farm, the death of a bird or any animal was always followed by a funeral. Children love dressing up and we became high-priests overnight so that we could bury our feathered friends with ceremony and what we considered the right rituals. They were sometimes slightly over the top, but, then, children love drama! Later, wooden crosses were erected to commemorate our friends.

The Robin's Cross

A little cross
To tell my loss;
A little bed
To rest my head;
A little tear is all I crave
Upon my very little grave.

I strew thy bed
Who loved thy lays;
The tear I shed;
The cross I raise,
With nothing more upon it than,
'Here lies the little friend of man.'

George Darley

Chapter 7

The Gift of Trees

Poems we learned in school peal forever like a faint bell in the echo chambers of our minds. Woven from creativity, they blend into our own pool of creativity and rest forever deep within us. We may forget the lessons of our schoolbooks, but not the poems, because poems are part of an essence that lifts us above the mundane in everyday living. They are the communication link that connects us to the divine and the natural world. Sometimes in life you are stopped in your tracks by something that holds you spellbound and is almost beyond your ability to absorb or describe – it is then the poet comes to your rescue. A poem pealing at first like a distant bell slowly comes closer and suddenly you and the poet are standing in the same shoes. These are the stand-out moments of life. And you are so happy that a poet has walked this path ahead of you and that her or his words

are still there on the back pages of your mind. The poet too has seen that flight of birds or that great tree and you are now walking in the same shoes. The wonder of nature and the majesty of great trees enriches our world, as indeed do the poets who have immersed themselves in this sacredness and grandeur, and passed their vision on to us.

Growing up surrounded by trees coloured our lives. My father was a planter of trees and as nature at the time was given free rein, it provided them naturally as well: some of the trees and hedges self-seeded along the ditches that were then the farm boundaries and supported a multiplicity of trees, bushes and briars. The birds also dropped their undigested seeds at random and little seedlings sprang up in unexpected places. In spreading seeds the birds were providing their future homes in the resulting rich habitat. This was the balance of nature in action. We became even more aware of it with this lesson at school.

Little by Little
'Little by Little,' an acorn said,
As it slowly sank in its mossy bed,
'I am improving every day,
Hidden deep in the earth away.'

Little by little, each day it grew,
Little by little, it sipped the dew,
Downward it sent out a thread-like root;
Up in the air sprung a tiny shoot.

Day after day, and year after year,
Little by little the leaves appear;
And the little branches spread far and wide,
Till the mighty oak is the forest's pride.

'Little by little,' said the thoughtful boy,
'Each precious moment I will employ,
And always this rule in my mind shall dwell:
Whatever I do, I'll do it well.

'Little by little, I'll learn to know
The treasured wisdom of long ago;
And sometime, perhaps, the world will be
Happier and better because of me.'

Anonymous

Going to school through the fields taught us many lessons. My father was constantly chanting the refrain 'Wrong nature and we will pay a terrible price', and it is only now that I realise what he meant. We have neglected the planting of trees and we have built on bogs and flood-plains, damaging our natural habitat and affecting our bird life. Great trees are the lungs of the earth, cleansing the air and drinking surplus water, and while doing all this are still majestic and beautiful. Is there anything more awe-inspiring than a great tree in the centre of a large field? Any time I notice one I am reminded of this poem from my school days, and it makes me much more appreciative.

Poem Lovely as a Tree
I think that I shall never see
A poem lovely as a tree.

A tree whose hungry mouth is prest
Against the earth's sweet flowing breast;

A tree that looks at God all day,
And lifts her leafy arms to pray;

A tree that may in Summer wear
A nest of robins in her hair;

Upon whose bosom snow has lain;
Who intimately lives with rain.

Poems are made by fools like me,
But only God can make a tree.

Joyce Kilmer

Here the creator and creation dance together. It was a great poem for rural children growing up surrounded by trees and nature. My father instilled a deep respect for trees in us, telling us that it takes a tree many, many years to grow, but a fool can cut it down in five minutes. He also believed that a person who planted a tree was far less likely to chop one down.

Those lessons that we learned in school at a very early age became imprinted on our young minds, never to be forgotten. Years later they came alive when certain scenes floated before us and awakened long-forgotten lines of poetry. When writing the following poem the poet was dancing with the delights of trees in autumn.

October's Party
October gave a party;
The leaves by hundreds came–
The Chestnuts, Oaks, and Maples,
The leaves of every name.

The sunshine spread a carpet,
And everything was grand,
Miss Weather led the dancing,
Professor Wind the band.

The Chestnuts came in Yellow,
The Oaks in crimson dressed;
The lovely Misses Maple
In scarlet looked their best.

All balanced to their partners,
And gaily fluttered by,
The sight was like a rainbow
New fallen from the sky.

George Cooper

Is there anything more beautiful than the woods in autumn? In Innishannon we are so lucky to be living in the wooded valley along the banks of the river Bandon, which stretches from the town of Bandon to Kinsale harbour. We owe a debt of gratitude to the people who went before us who had the foresight to leave such a rich heritage of trees. To drive along this valley is lovely at any time of the year but in the autumn the woods along this road are spectacular and their memory would sustain you through the bareness of winter.

Our primary school in the home place was also surrounded by fields and woods, so poems about trees at any time of year came alive around us, though more so in autumn. Here's one I particularly loved, possible because the 'children' refused initially to play their expected part. In this poem the parent tree is trying to put the children to bed, but like all children they want to hang on for a little bit longer.

How the Leaves Came Down
I'll tell you how the leaves came down:
The great Tree to his children said,
'You're getting sleepy, Yellow and Brown,
Yes, very sleepy, little Red;
It is quite time to go to bed.'
'Ah!' begged each silly, pouting leaf,
'Let us a little longer stay;
Dear Father Tree, behold our grief!
'Tis such a very pleasant day,
We do not want to go away.'

So, just for one more merry day
To the great Tree the leaflets clung,
Frolicked and danced and had their way,
Upon the autumn breezes swung,
Whispering all their sports among.

'Perhaps the great Tree will forget
And let us stay until the spring,
If we all beg and coax and fret.'
But the great Tree did no such thing;
He smiled to hear their whispering.

'Come, children all, to bed,' he cried;
And ere the leaves could urge their prayer,
He shook his head, and far and wide,
Fluttering and rustling everywhere,
Down sped the leaflets through the air.

Anonymous

Also hurrying the leaves down was the wind that began as a whisper in autumn but later turned into howling winter storms. These winds whirled through the leaves, loosening their grip, and, as they floated down, sped them on their way. As the whispering wind whirled around the trees he also whispered through our farmhouse, and at night when it whistled along the rafters we could imagine the Whisper-Whisper Man tossing the leaves about in the groves around the house.

The Whisper-Whisper Man

The whisper-whisper man
Makes all the wind in the world.
He has a gown as brown as brown;
His hair is long and curled.

In the stormy winter-time
He taps at your window-pane,
And all the night, until it's light
He whispers through the rain.

If you peeped through a Fairy Ring
You'd see him, little and brown;
You'd hear the beat of his clackety feet,
Scampering through the town.

But when the whispering autumn wind turned into a raging winter storm we listened in awe as it howled through the trees and rattled the windows and doors of the house. When the trees groaned in protest my father worried that one would be uprooted and come down on top of us. But it never happened because our house was in the sheltered corner of a south-facing hill. But as a child, with no such adult worry about the danger of storms, it was lovely to listen to the wind tossing the trees about and whistling through the house. In those days, with no insulation of windows and doors, the wind had free access to us.

The Wind

Why does the wind so want to be
Here in my little room with me?
He's all the world to blow about,
But just because I keep him out
He cannot be a moment still
But frets upon my window-sill,
And sometimes brings a noisy rain
To help him batter at the pane.

Upon my door he comes to knock.
He rattles, rattles at the lock
And lifts the latch and stirs the key–
Then waits a moment breathlessly,
And soon, more fiercely than before,
He shakes my little trembling door,
And though 'Come in, Come in!' I say,
He neither comes nor goes away.

Elizabeth Rendall

It was lovely to cuddle up in a warm bed listening to the wind howling around the house, rattling the windows and doors and sometimes blowing out the candle, and with their words the poets painted these images on the canvas of our minds and created scenes that remained with us for the rest of our lives.

Chapter 8

Tick-tock!

There is something very comforting about the ticking of a clock. I have a few ticking clocks and when I forget to wind them I soon miss the tick-tock. Each of my ticking clocks has its own story. One was the post-office clock in the village when I came here in 1961. Uncle Jacky and Aunty Peg, who ran the post office, were given it when they got married in 1932 by the Valley Rovers, the local GAA club with which Jacky was involved all his life. Over the years it has got a few life-saving overhauls by understanding clock repairers, whose correct title I have learned is 'horologist'. Uncle Jacky's clock has a calming tick-tock and a lovely, soothing chime. It now has pride of place on Aunty Peg's old sideboard in my front room. Another clock I have was rescued came from a dump and it now hangs over the fireplace in the Seomra Ciúin. When its many coats of dead

"Now who was
?" he asked
Michael.
You are work-
now," said I
"but I
hat you
ain

Big Hand. "I have
I have years
Michael.
ck-tock

43

paint were stripped off, a beautiful inlaid mahogany surface was uncovered. This is an ancient eight-day clock that needs winding only once a week. These eight-day clocks need to be perfectly balanced to keep going and keep the correct time. The first step in achieving this is a wall whose contours suit the clock, because while a clock may happily tick away on one wall it could stubbornly and silently refuse to keep going on another. Once the wall and the clock are compatible, the clock then needs to be hung in a manner that keeps the pendulum swinging back and forth in perfect balance. Ascertaining this balance may take time and constant checking that the pendulum is hanging properly off the hook high up in the interior of the clock. This hook is not visible from the outside so the horologist has to be guided by touch-and-feel control. This is a skill acquired through years of experience. Once perfect location and pendulum balance are achieved, the wall beside it may then be marked by pencil and were the clock ever to be moved from its desired moorings the pencil mark guarantees perfect relocation. This is a simple method learnt from my father many years ago when we had a similar clock hanging in our kitchen. These clocks, even though common in Ireland at the time of my childhood, were made in America, but bought locally after a lot of serious consideration because they were quite expensive and a big family investment. On the farm they were almost looked on as an additional pleasant piece of furniture rather than time-keepers because people reared on the land had developed a natural ability while out in the fields of telling the time of day by the location of the sun. One old man who worked with us always said that on standing in the centre of a field at any time of the year he could know the month of the year, the day of the week and the exact time of day. He then added that the introduction of the clock destroyed this ability.

My father had a big silver watch in its own case that hung from a chain in his waistcoat pocket which he consulted when Big Ben pealed out from the BBC. As a child I thought that he was checking if Big Ben was right! My mother had a little gold wristwatch that she had got when getting married, but she seldom wore it, which was not surprising because time-keeping did not intrude into my mother's world. For us children watches were away above and beyond our aspirations and we were astute enough not to have one on our wants list – but that did not stop us from dreaming. I remember looking longingly at a watch in the window of a small shop in town and was so overpowered by my desire for acquisition that I tentatively mentioned the possibility of acquiring it to my father, who lost no time in telling me that it was way outside the bounds of possibility. So, early in life we were introduced to the word 'No', or as my grandmother put it 'mastering the art of the do-without', which probably later fostered a deep sense of appreciation and anticipation in us. When an older sister decided to go into nursing, the acquisition of a watch with a second hand was the cause of great wonder and made for delightful inspection by us younger ones. My grandmother had a weights and chains clock, which to me was intriguing, and at night I watched with fascination as she pulled down the chains, which bore the weights upwards to begin their descent again. Our neighbour Bill had a tall, elegant window clock, the winding of which was a major undertaking and if we happened to be present he had an appreciative audience.

So maybe it is not surprising that I inherited a fascination with clocks, though not necessarily for their time-keeping ability. Over the Aga in the kitchen is my favourite clock from which the Big Ben chimes peal forth every quarter-hour, and on the hour it gives the appropriate full toll. In childhood these chimes boomed forth daily on our battery radio as my father waited to be informed by the BBC as to how the world was managing its affairs.

Another clock, given to my daughter on her twenty-first birthday by our cousin Con (custodian of some of these old books), sits on the piano. I am the caretaker of this clock until her little ones can resist the temptation to investigate its inner mechanisms. Another eight-day clock in the kitchen was purchased by Con at an antique fair many years ago. This venerable oak model has only the tick-tock voice as the hourly chiming voice has ceased to function, which is just as well as it was rasp rather than a chime. Down the corridor, lying on its back in a spare room, is another eight-day clock, waiting to have its life restored by my brilliant horologist, who has retired but keeps all his neighbours' clocks ticking. Currently he is engaged in breathing life into a grandfather clock that Gabriel and I purchased to mark the arrival of the new millennium. In case you think that this grandfather clock is a magnificent creation in mahogany, forget it! It's a battered old boy made of oak that has to be balanced with a few books to keep it level – and ticking. But we happened on it in a second-hand furniture shop when the country was alive with millennium mania and decided that it was a good way to mark the passage of time. Over the last twenty years it has become a friendly presence standing in the corner of the front room. At the moment its innards have gone for an overhaul and I am looking forward to their return. You miss the presence of a clock that has been a companion for a long period.

In case you think from all of this meandering on about clocks that I am a good time-keeper, not at all! Each clock has a different story and it's all about the story! Here's a song we learned as children, which was part of our home and school, as all of us loved it and sang it a lot!

My Grandfather's Clock
My grandfather's clock was too large for the shelf,
So it stood ninety years on the floor.
It was taller by half than the old man himself,
Though it weighed not a pennyweight more.
It was bought on the morn of the day that he was
    born,
And was always his treasure and pride;
But it stopped short – never to go again –
When the old man died.

Ninety years without slumbering
(tick, tock, tick, tock),
His life's seconds numbering,
(tick, tock, tick, tock),
It stopped short – never to go again –
When the old man died.

In watching its pendulum swing to and fro,
Many hours had he spent while a boy;
And in childhood and manhood the clock seemed to
      know
And to share both his grief and his joy.
For it struck twenty-four when he entered at the door
With a blooming and beautiful bride;
But it stopped short – never to go again –
When the old man died.

My grandfather said that of those he could hire,
Not a servant so faithful he found,
For it wasted no time, and had but one desire –
At the close of each week to be wound.
And it kept in its place – not a frown upon its face,
And its hands never hung by its side,
But it stopped short – never to go again –
When the old man died.

It rang an alarm in the dead of the night –
An alarm that for years had been dumb;

And we knew that his spirit was pluming for flight –
That his hour of departure had come.
Still the clock kept the time, with a soft and muffled
chime,
As we silently stood by his side;
But it stopped short – never to go again –
When the old man died.

The winding of our clock took place every Saturday night at half-past ten, carried out by my father on his way to bed. It was part of his departing ritual from downstairs where my mother was just beginning to get going on her usual late-night burst of delayed activities, which he acknowledged with his departing words as he put his foot on the first step of the stairs: 'See you before morning, Missus.' My mother's name was Lena, and when they were singing from the same hymn sheet that became Len, but when they were swimming in different directions it changed to Missus. He was an early bird and she was a night owl, and ne'er the twain did meet.

First having listened to the News and then the Hospitals' Sweepstakes programme, when Bart Bastable assured us 'makes no difference where you are, you can wish upon a star', my father went to the clock and, easing back its glass front door, he opened the smaller door beneath it and reached his fingers down into its interiors to fish out a brass key, which he then edged, in turn, into each side of the clock face and wound it slowly in regular circular turns. Then he replaced the key inside the little glass door at the bottom and closed the circular door at the front, and the clock ticked away happily for another week. Because my father held our clock in such reverence we children were under pain of extinction were we to touch it, but occasionally he would remove the cover of his own pocket-watch and show us its amazingly complex interior. The whole world of time-keeping was an absolute wonder to me. No surprise then that to me 'The Watchmaker's Shop' in our schoolbook was an Aladdin's cave of mystery.

The Watchmaker's Shop
A street in our town
Has a queer little shop
With tumble-down walls
And a thatch on the top;
And all the wee windows
With crookedy panes
Are shining and winking
With watches and chains.

(All sorts and all sizes
In silver and gold,
And brass ones and tin ones
And new ones and old;
And clocks for the kitchen
And clocks for the hall,
High ones and low ones
And wag-at-the-wall.)

The watchmaker sits
On a long-legged seat
And bids you the time
Of the day when you meet;
And round and about him
There's ticketty-tock
From the tiniest watch
To the grandfather clock.

I wonder he doesn't
Get tired of the chime
And all the clocks ticking
And telling the time;
But there he goes winding
Lest any should stop,
This queer little man
In the watchmaker's shop.

There is something fascinating about a shop such as the above and they are now a rare presence on any street. But there is one (although admittedly a much posher one than in the poem) along a street in Cork and it is difficult to pass by without peering through the window or popping in to have a look and a listen. In there is an incredible collection of grandfather clocks – and of course the grandfather clock is the *crème de la crème* of clocks. It is lovely to loiter around looking at the interesting faces and waiting to hear the different chiming and tolling of the hours. Every clock is in perfect nick and each is busy going about its business, but of course it is the grandfathers who are the top brass, smiling down on all the others.

The Grandfather Clock
Our clock has such a merry face,
And from his corner in the hall
He watches me go in and out,
Upstairs and down I hear his call.

He tells me when 'tis time to rise,
He rings so loudly when it's eight,
And, oh, I'm sure he looks at me
When I come down to breakfast late.

And even if I wake at night,
All in the lonely dark, I hear
The dear old clock who never sleeps,
And feel as if a friend is near.

Lucy Diamond

An amusing little story in one of our schoolbooks brought the grandfather clock to life for me. I could perfectly understand how Michael the mouse was so upset when the clock stopped because if our kitchen clock came to a standstill my father lost his head – to be honest it did not always require such a rare event as the stopped clock to trigger off this reaction! But, maybe with an easy-going wife and seven children who were forever upsetting the balance of his life, and helpers who did not always get his instructions on first hearing, to my father the clock was a calm, dependable, regular rhythm in his sometimes chaotic household. Not that he ever depended on it to tell the time as he had an innate sense of that from his long years of working on the land, but to my father the clock represented a certain sense of dependability and law and order, and, like Michael the mouse, when it stopped his balance was upset. So to me, in this story Michael and my father became one.

When the Clock Stopped

One night, when everyone in the house was asleep, the big clock in the hall stopped.

Michael the mouse wondered what was wrong, so he came out from his hole and said:

'This will never do. Why have you stopped, Mr. Clock? I am so used to your tick-tock, tick-tock that I feel quite lonely without it.'

'Don't blame me,' said the clock. 'It is all the Big Hand's fault.'

'What is wrong, Big Hand?' asked Michael. 'Why have you stopped?'

'I'm tired,' said the Big Hand, 'and I don't see why I should have to travel so much faster than the Hour Hand. So I'm taking a rest to myself.'

Now Michael was a very wise little mouse. He thought for a moment, and then he said:

'I am sorry for you, Big Hand, tomorrow you will be cast

into the box under the stairs, and a bright new hand will take your place. You are old and worn-out.'

'How dare you speak to me like that!' said the Big Hand. 'I am neither old nor worn-out. Believe me, my long-tailed friend, I am as young as ever I was.'

'If you hadn't stopped,' went on Michael, 'I fully believe the Hour Hand would have overtaken you.'

'That is nonsense,' said the Big Hand. 'Watch! I can still travel as fast as ever.'

The Big Hand went off at such a rate that he soon made up for the time he had lost.

'Now who was right?' he asked Michael.

'You are working well now,' said Michael, 'but I know well that you will grow tired again in a little while.'

'Not I!' said the Big Hand. 'I have never felt better in my life. I have years and years of ticking in me.'

'I am very glad to hear it,' said Michael. 'I felt very lonely when your tick-tock stopped.

'By the way,' he went on then, 'have you seen the cat lately?'

'I think she is asleep on the mat outside the hall door,' said the Big Hand.

'Good!' said Michael the mouse. 'I think I'll go down to the pantry to get some cheese.'

Some clocks have a lovely chime and there is something very pleasant about that sound. Perhaps electric ones are better time-keepers, but life is not all about time-keeping. Timothy knew that at a very young age and so did we, and we could identify with every step that Timothy took on his way to and from school because his journey, like ours, was full of distractions from the destination that he and we should have had in mind. But if we did not take the time to check the eggs in the birds' nest that had little cracks on them the day before, we might miss the arrival of the baby chicks. Also, on the way to school we were on the constant lookout for bulls that might hurry us to our final end, and sometimes made long circuits to avoid what were probably harmless cows. Watching the water hens in the river and catching tadpoles were far more interesting activities than anything we might learn in school. So I could understand Timothy's dilemma very well and I was on his side.

Lost Time
Timothy took his time to school,
Plenty of time he took;
But some he lost in the tadpole pool,
And some in the stickle-back brook.
Ever so much in the linnet's nest,
And more on the five-barred gate –
Timothy took his time to school
But he lost it all and was late.

Timothy has a lot to do –
How shall it all be done?
Why, he never got home till close on two,
Though he might have been home by one.
There's sums, and writing and spelling too,

And an apple tree to climb.
Timothy has a lot to do –
How shall he find the time?

Timothy sought it high and low;
He looked in the tadpole pool,
To see if they'd taken the time to grow,
That he lost on the way to school.
He found the nest, and he found the tree,
And he found the gate he'd crossed
But Timothy never shall find (ah me!)
The time that Timothy lost.

Ffrida Wolfe

Didn't Timothy have a wonderful time as he journeyed to school? And there was another little boy in our schoolbook – Johnny – who was not too worried about time either. He was a bit like my friend Denny. Denny lived along our valley so we all journeyed together back and forth to school. Denny loved looking at the sky and would often get us all to lie down on the warm grass to look up and admire the clouds. All these extra-curricular activities did not lend themselves to punctuality, but as we approached the school gate an awareness of lateness asserted itself, and we opened the classroom door with a certain amount of apprehension because if we had overrun a particular deadline and were marked absent on the massive tome known as the Roll Book that would be the cause of serious concern. To whom it might cause concern, I am not quite sure, but in our world the Master who called the rolls was the nearest thing to God. There was a small, shiny alarm clock on the window of the classroom, but the Master had a long, silver watch-chain draping out of his pocket and when he withdrew this as you arrived in class and peered down at it disapprovingly, you sensed that you had broken one of the Ten Commandments, which was a big deal in our world. So, in order not to offend God, we were aware that a certain amount of speed was sometimes advisable. But all our sympathies were with Johnny and in spirit we wanted to issue words of caution as he approached the river. We also had a river on our way to school and it too was the source of endless distractions, so we understood Johnny's dilemma very well.

Johnny
As he trudged along to school,
It was always Johnny's rule
To be looking at the sky
And the clouds that floated by;
But what just before him lay
In his way,
Johnny never thought about;
So that everyone cried out:
'Look at little Johnny there,
Little Johnny head-in-air!'

Running just in Johnny's way,
Came a little dog one day;
Johnny eyes were still astray
Up on high,
In the sky
And he never heard them cry
'Johnny, mind, the dog is nigh!'

Once, with head as high as ever,
Johnny walked beside the river.
Johnny watched the swallows trying
Which was cleverest at flying.
Oh! what fun!
Johnny watched the bright round sun
Coming in and coming out;
This was all he thought about.

So he strode on, only think!
To the river's very brink
Where the bank was high and steep
And the water very deep;
And the fishes, in a row,
Stared to see him coming so.
One step more! Oh, sad to tell!
Headlong in poor Johnny fell,
And the fishes in dismay
Wagged their tails and swam away.

There lay Johnny on his face,
With his nice red writing case;
But, as they were passing by,
Two strong men had heard him cry;
And with sticks, these two strong men
Hooked poor Johnny out again.

Oh! you should have seen him shiver
When they pulled him from the river.
He was in a sorry plight!
Dripping wet, and such a fright!
Wet all over, everywhere,
Clothes, and arms, and face, and hair.
Johnny never will forget
What it is to be so wet.

And the fishes, one, two, three,
Are come back again, you see;
Up they come the moment after
To enjoy the fun and laughter.
Each popped out his little head
And to tease poor Johnny said:
'Silly little Johnny, look,
You have lost your writing book!'

T.H. Hoffman

I thought that it was so mean of the fish to be laughing at poor Johnny because in many ways Johnny was *us*. Did we learn anything from Johnny's tardiness? Not really! I just loved him and was full of sympathy and understanding for both Johnny and Timothy. They were our soulmates!

Chapter 9

Farm Friends

Like every farmer's wife of the time my mother was a great fowl woman. She kept hens, guinea hens, ducks, geese, and eventually turkeys when they arrived in rural Ireland. At first the turkey was regarded as a step above the goose, but now roast goose is deemed to be a greater speciality. The male turkeys and geese were aggressive in defence of their young, which is why we children preferred the ducks. The drake was far more kindly and this gave us a chance to handle the baby ducks, who were gorgeous fluffy little bundles. We loved the ducks and of course this poem in our schoolbook was a firm favourite.

Michael Met a White Duck
Michael met a white duck
Walking on the green,

ET A WHITE DUCK

a white duck

green,

" said Mich

eather'

'How are you?' said Michael,
'How fine the weather's been!
Blue sky and sunshine
All through the day;
Not a single raindrop
Came to spoil our play.'

But the sad white duck said,
'I myself want rain,
I'd like to see the brooklets
And the streams fill up again.
Now I can't go swimming,
It really makes me cry
To see the little duckponds
Look so very dry.'

J. Dupuy

When we learned this lesson in our schoolbook the biggest
duck in our flock was immediately christened Michael. But
our ducks, unlike Michael's white duck, had no shortage of
water because it constantly tumbled down from a glen in the
fields behind the house. That flow of water was not quite a river,
but it was quite a robust stream; it was referred to as a '*glaishe*', the
Irish word for 'stream'. We had many such *glaishes* around the
farm and all eventually found their way down to the river that
flowed along the valley below us, which formed the boundary
with the neighbouring farm. It was lovely to watch the ducks
enjoying themselves in the water.

Ducks' Ditty

All along the backwater,
Through the rushes tall,
Ducks are a-dabbling,
Up tails all!

Ducks' tails, drakes' tails,
Yellow feet a-quiver,
Yellow bills all out of sight
Busy in the river!

Slushy green undergrowth
Where the roach swim –
Here we keep our larder
Cool and full and dim!

Everyone for what he likes!
We like to be
Heads down, tails up,
Dabbling free!

High in the blue above
Swift whirl and call –
We are down a-dabbling,
Up tails all!

Kenneth Grahame

Unfortunately geese and ducks are not very hygiene conscious and my father had big questions about their over-use of the *glaishes* and river as he worried that they would pollute the water. A keen fisherman, he would walk along the river bank and check the quality of the water coming into it off the land. The river was a source of constant delight for us. In summer we swam in it and caught 'collies' in jampots. It was full of brown trout which my father brought home on Sunday evenings after an afternoon fishing. We knew that salmon came up there to spawn and this lesson in our schoolbook filled us in on the details.

The Salmon

The sea is the salmon's home, but the river is its nursery. Not that young salmon get much nursing; indeed from babyhood they have to look after themselves.

When the mother salmon wants to lay her eggs she leaves the sea and goes up a river.

In the sandy river bed she scoops a hole with her tail, and in it she lays a few hundred smooth round eggs. Moving on to another place, she does the same again.

She continues this work for three or four days. Then she and her mate, leaving the eggs to hatch, drift lazily down the river back to the sea.

Many of the eggs are devoured by greedy brown trout and black eels. Those that escape hatch out in a few months into tiny fish.

The baby salmon is less than an inch long and as clear as glass. Under his chin is a little sack, like a horse's nose-bag, which holds enough food to keep him alive for some weeks.

He hides in a dark corner under a stone till his food is used up and hunger drives him out to look for more.

His early days are full of danger. He has many enemies – caddis worms, dragon-fly grubs with their cruel pincers, newts, water-beetles, and, of course, fish much bigger and stronger than himself.

But if he is lucky enough to live he soon becomes quite a handsome young fellow, some ten inches long, with a beautiful white waistcoat and a dark green mottled suit of scales.

By the time he is two years old he is nearly ten inches long and has got a new suit, this time of shining silver and blue.

And now he becomes very restless. He is no longer contented in the dark weedy river pools with the brown red-spotted trout for company. He swims to and fro uneasily.

Then, little by little every day, he begins to drop down the river towards the sea from which his parents came.

The fact that the young salmon make their way back home to their birthing river to spawn is one of the miracles of nature.

The river and the farm taught us many things and because the farm was our food chain we were very aware that in order to survive through the winter one had to work during the summer, so we understood very well the dilemma of the poor cricket in the following poem.

The Ant and the Cricket

A silly young cricket, accustomed to sing

Through the warm sunny months of gay summer and
    spring,

Began to complain, when he found that at home

His cupboard was empty and winter was come.

Not a crumb to be found

On the snow-covered ground;

Not a flower could he see,

Not a leaf on a tree:

'Oh what will become,' says the cricket, 'of me?'

At last by starvation and famine made bold,

All dripping with wet and all trembling with cold,

Away he set off to a miserly ant,

To see if, to keep him alive, he would grant

Him shelter from rain;

A mouthful of grain

He wished only to borrow,

He'd repay it to-morrow;

If not he must die of starvation and sorrow.

Says the ant to the cricket: 'I'm your servant and friend,

But we ants never borrow, we ants never lend;

But tell me, dear sir, did you lay nothing by

When the weather was warm?' Said the cricket: 'Not I.

My heart was so light

That I sang day and night,

For all nature looked gay.'

'You *sang* sir, you say?

Go then,' said the ant, 'and dance winter away.'

Thus ending, he hastily lifted the wicket

And out of the door turned the poor little cricket.

Though this is a fable, the moral is good:

If you live without work, you must live without food.

Wasn't that ant a pretty miserable old sod! One would not like to be living next door to him in a famine. As children we were very familiar with ants because any time we lifted up a stone in the our yard or garden, scores of them ran in all directions, and we believed that if you sat on an ants' nest they would swarm up your legs and sting you to death. We called them by the old name for them, 'pismires'; I leave it to your imagination …

So we did not have a very warm relationship with ants, whereas the cricket was a different story altogether. We never actually saw the cricket, but every night as we sat around the fire the cricket serenaded us from somewhere behind the bellows. We loved the sound and felt that the poor old cricket got a raw deal from the miserly old ant. His work was in entertainment, after all. It wasn't as if he did nothing!

But to us the bees in the hives were far more interesting and productive than the ants. My beekeeping brother had many hives from which came a constant supply of honey, so the world of the bees was a source of great fascination to us, and a lesson about them in our schoolbook extended our knowledge.

The Honey Bee

It is sometimes said of a person that he is 'as busy as a bee.' The honey bee is, indeed, one of the busiest little creatures in the world, and one of the most useful to man. She spends long days in spring and summer, going from flower to flower, gathering the nectar which will be turned into golden honey and stored in the hive.

With her long, hollow tongue she sups the nectar from the flowers and collects it in a little bag in her body called the *honey sac*. When her honey sac is full, she flies home to empty it, and then goes back to field or garden to her task of filling it again. Amongst the flowers she likes best to visit are the hawthorn, clover, heather, and apple blossom. She needs only a small part of the honey for her daily food. Most of it is put away safely for the winter, when nectar is hard to find.

The honey is stored in combs made of wax which she produces from her own body. They consist of a great number of cells, very regular in shape, each with six sides. The bee is, in fact, not only a honey-maker, but a very clever builder. Each cell, when filled, is carefully closed with a tiny cap of wax.

Bees like to live together in big families. If left to themselves, they will make their home in a tree or chimney, or under a roof, or in a hole in a wall. But they are quite happy to be presented with a hive. The bee-keeper even provides them with sheets of wax as a beginning for their combs, thus saving them much time and toil. In return he may get as much as one hundred pounds of honey in a season from a single stock of bees. The honey he takes away he must, of course, replace with other food which will keep the bees alive during the winter.

In the hive each working bee has its special duties. Some are sentries guarding the door of the hive against strangers. Others are nurses, to look after the young, and feed and keep them from harm. Others are there to receive the honey that is brought in and to put it away in the cells. And then there are the honey-gatherers themselves.

Over them all is a queen whose work it is to lay the eggs from which new bees will come.

In the bee world the female and the workers reign supreme, and at the end of the season, when the male drones are surplus to requirements, they are tossed out of the hive. As a child I felt that this was pretty tough on the poor old drones, but my brother loved his bees and to him the rules of the hive were above reproach.

The Little Red Hen was thinking along similar lines to the ant. She believed in equal rights for women and was compassionate as well. Though she had the same thinking as the ant, she somehow got her point across in a kinder way.

Little Red Hen
Once a Rat and Cat and Red Hen grew fat
In the hollow oak of a grassy glen:
'Let us have a feast fit for an Eastern king,
The like of which never was seen by men!
Let us haste and make

A dark speckled cake
With plums from the lands of the Saracen!'
'Let us!' says Rat. 'Let us!' says Cat.
'Let us make the cake!' says Little Red Hen.

'Who will go to the mill by the mountain rill
That tumbles o'er rocks to our grassy glen;
And get wheat ground as the wheel goes round,
Then sifted and sacked by the miller's men;
That we three may make
Our dark speckled cake
With plums from the lands of the Saracen?'
'I won't!' says Rat. 'I won't!' says Cat.
'I'll do it myself!' says Little Red Hen.

'Who will elbows bare and will apron wear,
And mix the dough with a housewife's ken?
Who will round the cake and set it to bake,
And watch that it may not blacken or bren?
Who will undertake
To bespeck this cake
With plums from the lands of Saracen?'
'I won't!' says Rat. 'I won't!' says Cat.
'I'll do it myself!' says Little Red Hen.

'Who will take high seat with neckerchief neat,
White coifed like the wives of great gentlemen?
Who will bend a face at saying of grace,

And at the end of the blessing will say Amen?
Who will eat the cake
That myself shall bake
With plums from the lands of the Saracen?'
'I will!' says Rat. 'I will!' says Cat.
'I'll eat it myself!' says Little Red Hen.

M. J. McCall

The life and animals in our schoolbooks came alive around
the farmyard. One of the fluffiest and most industrious of
my mother's Rhode Island Red hens was immediately identified as the Little Red Hen and because she was always
busy scratching around the yard providing for her chicks, it
was easy to see that she was an industrious little lady who
was always getting things done. She was a picture of self-
sufficiency who would soon put manners on the rat and the
cat, because nobody would be allowed to loiter around our
busy little red hen. But we had no sympathy for the cat and
the rat in the poem because we knew all about sharing the
work load, as we had long lists of allocated jobs to be done
around the house and the yard and nobody got away with
dodging the issue. I hated 'the jobs', but there was no getting away from them because we children were part of the
work force that kept the wheels turning. My mother was
not a hard taskmaster, but older sisters made sure that you
got away with nothing, and if you chanced your arm and
tried to dodge the jobs you were soon called to order. You
were immediately charged with being a 'dodger', which was

a highly undesirable title. So when I read *Oliver Twist* for the first time and discovered the Artful Dodger, I was surprised and delighted to discover one in there as well.

But the fact that we were so involved with the farm work meant that we got to know the animals very well and loved the baby chicks, lambs, goslings and ducks. We had Larry the lamb, Curly Wee the baby bonham and Richey the pet calf. Some of these who were too frail to survive out in the yard were brought indoors to be hand-fed and nurtured, and we became their foster mothers. So all the poems and lessons in our schoolbooks dealing with wild life and animals blended seamlessly into our way of life.

Chapter 10

Storytelling

At night when the lessons were done and the books back in the school sacks, our neighbour Bill told us stories. Some he made up as he went along and others were old myths and legends. It made no difference to us because there were no boundaries between reality and fantasy in our world. One story that we particularly loved was the story of the Salmon of Knowledge. From school we were familiar with tales about Fionn and the Fianna, but the Salmon of Knowledge as Bill told it had special appeal – he was wonderful storyteller with great big hands that he used to illustrate points; if he added too many extras and flourishes we soon brought him back on track, but if he told it very dramatically we went along happily with that. With the capacity of children to listen to the same story again and again, we never got tired of the Salmon of Knowledge. Here it is as I remember it from Bill.

The story began with Finnegas, who was one of the wisest people in Ireland but had a thirst for more knowledge. He had heard of an ancient well around which grew nine hazel trees and one day the wind blew the hazel nuts into the well and a salmon swallowed them up. He was filled with knowledge and became known as the Salmon of Knowledge.

Finnegas heard of the Salmon of Knowledge and moved to live beside the well in the hope of catching and sampling the salmon, because it was said that the first person to taste the Salmon of Knowledge would become the wisest person in Ireland. This became the dream of Finnegas.

At that time young warriors had to be wise as well as brave and were sent to study with wise women and men like Finnegas, and so it was that Fionn of the Fianna was sent to be taught by Finnegas all the wisdom that he had. Finnegas never told Fionn about the Salmon of Knowledge and every day he went to fish in the deep well, hoping to catch the salmon.

But this was a very clever salmon and for a long time was too smart for Finnegas. But one day Finnegas was lucky and after a long struggle he landed the Salmon of Knowledge! He was delighted but exhausted and so asked Fionn to cook the salmon, warning him not to taste it. Fionn was an honourable young man and Finnegas knew that he could trust him. And so, while the exhausted Finnegas slept, Fionn cooked the salmon. During the cooking a blister rose on the back of the salmon which Fionn pressed down with his thumb, and, taken by surprise at the sudden pain, he licked his finger.

When the dinner was ready Fionn called Finnegas and they sat down to eat. Finnegas tasted the salmon and was surprised that nothing unusual seemed to happen to him. Then he looked at Fionn and saw a difference in him, so he asked Fionn if he had tasted the salmon. Fionn said no, but then he remembered the blister and his sore thumb. Finnegas was disappointed, but knew that it was an honest mistake.

So Fionn became the wisest man in Ireland.

We loved Bill's stories about people who had lived long, long before our time. Fionn and the Fianna were the source of endless wonder, as indeed was Cuchulainn. This is a story about Cuchulainn from one of our schoolbooks. We loved it because it was about horses, and this held a special relevance for us as horses were part of our daily lives. Now, admittedly, our horses fell well short of Cuchulainn's colourful steeds, but the one thing that we did not lack was imagination. So as the story unfolded our two hairy-legged farm horses out in the stable were transformed into the Grey of Macha and the Black Steed of the Glen.

How Cuchulainn Got His Horses

While Cuchulainn was still a little lad he went to Shadow Land, where there lived a wise warrior-woman called Scath, to be taught the feats of skill that a soldier should know. For a day and a year he stayed with her, and learnt all that she could teach him. The last two things that she taught him, and the most difficult of all, were how to thrust with a spear and how to cross a bridge in two leaps.

It was on the night of his return to Eire from Shadow Land that he caught his two chariot horses, the Grey of Macha, and the Black Steed of the Glen, and this is how he caught them.

He was passing along the borders of the Grey Lake that
is near the mountain of Slieve Fuad, thinking of the life that
was to be his as a soldier. Slowly he walked along the reedy,
marshy ground that lay beside the lake, till he saw a mist rise
from the water and cover all the plain. Then, as he stood to
watch, he saw the form of a mighty horse, grey and weird
and phantom-like, rise slowly from the centre of the lake and
draw near to the shore, until it stood with its back to him
among the rushes of the water's edge.

Softly Cuchulainn crept down behind the horse; but it
seemed not to hear him come, for it was looking out towards
the centre of the lake. Then with a sudden leap Cuchulainn
was on its neck, his two hands clasped upon its mane. When
it felt the rider on its back, the noble animal shuddered from
head to foot, and started back and tried to throw Cuchulainn;
but with all his might he clung and would not be thrown.

Then began a struggle of champions between the hero and
the horse. All night they wrestled, and the prancing of the
horse was heard at King Conor's palace of Emain Macha, so
that the warriors said it thundered and that a great storm of
wind had arisen.

But when it could by no means throw Cuchulainn from
its back, the horse began to career and course round the
island, and that night they sped with the swiftness of the wind
three times round all the provinces of Ireland. With a bound
the wild creature leaped the mountains, and the sound of its
hoofs over the plains was like the breaking of the tempestu-
ous surf upon the shore.

Only once did they halt in their career, and that was in the wild and lonely glen in Donegal that is called the Black Glen where the ocean waves roll inward to the land.

From out of the waters arose another horse, as black as night, and it neighed to the Grey of Macha, so that the Grey of Macha stopped, and the Black Steed of the Glen came up and trotted by its side. Then the fury of the Grey of Macha ceased, and Cuchulainn could feel beneath his hand that the two horses were obedient to his will.

He brought them home to Emain and harnessed them to his chariot, and all the men of Ulster marvelled at the splendour of those horses, which were like night and day, the dark horse and the light. The grey horse they called the Grey of Macha, because Macha was the goddess of war and combat, and the other they called the Black Steed of the Glen.

Eleanor Hull

We wanted to bring these magnificent horses to life on paper and even though there was no drawing or painting on the school curriculum, that did not suppress our irrepressible urge to illustrate these amazing steeds galloping along our valley with their extraordinary chariots in tow. The fact that we had never even seen a chariot did nothing to quell our enthusiasm to whip one into being. Colouring pencils and crayons were a scarce commodity, but sometimes Santa came good and the crayons and pencils he brought were hoarded and used sparingly on the unused back pages of old copybooks, or indeed occasionally along the margins of our books. These artistic pursuits on the margins were not encouraged, although sometimes similar efforts by previous owners were already evident.

Fionn and the Fianna, and Superman Cuchulain, were some of the bridges by which we travelled back thousands of years into the past where we met ancestors from another age, and once we were back there in the mists of time anything was possible. It seemed like a magical time and the poems in particular brought that past to life.

The Song of Inisfail
They came from a land beyond the sea,
And now o'er the western main
Set sail, in their good ships, gallantly,
From the sunny land of Spain.
'Oh, where's the Isle we've seen in dreams,
Our destined home or grave?' –
Thus sang they, as by the morning's beams
They swept the Atlantic wave.

And, lo, where afar o'er ocean shines
A sparkle of radiant green,
As though in that deep lay emerald mines,
Whose light through the wave was seen.
''Tis Inisfail – 'tis Inisfail!'
Rings o'er the echoing sea;
While, bending to heaven, the warriors hail
That home of the brave and free.

Then turned they unto the eastern wave,
Where now their Day-God's eye
A look of such sunny omen gave
As lighted up sea and sky.
Nor frown was seen through sky or sea,
Nor tear o'er leaf or sod,
When first on their Isle of Destiny
Our great forefathers trod.

Thomas Moore

As we learned that poem it was easy to imagine these mighty warriors in huge sailing ships breasting the waves towards Ireland. And many other stories in our schoolbooks were about these people and their successors. It was difficult to know where reality ended and myths and legends began, but all painted pictures of an Ireland long, long before our time.

Long, Long Ago

Long, long ago there came to Ireland the Celts, a race of tall fair-haired men who were hardy fighters. They made themselves masters of the land, and settled down to live in it. Their houses were mostly built of wood, whitened with lime on the outside, and thatched with straw or rushes.

The Celts were pagans; they worshipped the sun, moon and stars, and pillars of wood and stone which they themselves set up. Their priests, the Druids, built their altars under oak trees.

They were a people fond of music and stories, and they honoured the men who made their stories and songs. These men – the Bards, as they were called – came next in rank to kings and chiefs, and were allowed to wear very gay clothes. A king sometimes wore seven different colours, and a Bard or a Druid six.

The Celts were skilful workers in metal. They knew how to mine the copper that is found in Cork and Waterford, and to mix it with tin so as to get bronze. They made tools and weapons of iron. They also fashioned crowns, collars, brooches, and other beautiful things of gold. Traders came from Spain and Gaul – now France – to buy silver and copper-work from Ireland.

When a number of Celtic families bearing the same name lived near one another, they formed what was called a clan, under the rule of a chief. The chiefs had to obey the kings of their provinces, and over all the kings was the Ard Ri or High King.

Every third year the High King held a great meeting on the holy hill of Tara. The laws were given out. There were all sorts of games and contests, and the Bards told new stories and taught new songs. This was the famous Feis of Tara.

We were fascinated by the idea of such a different world where even the men wore colourful clothes! That to us was almost unbelievable because in our day, clothes were fairly dull and ordinary – functional – especially for boys and men. We could not imagine my father or my brother wearing seven different colours. Or gold collars. Or brooches! The old world seemed like an extraordinary place and painted a picture of a colourful and ostentatious world where men adorned themselves like the peacocks that we saw in books or the cock pheasants out in the meadows, whose beautiful rich feathers were an awe-inspiring sight.

A love of and pride in our country was fostered throughout our school years. Ireland of the 1940s was a very different place to nowadays; it was only twenty years after independence and we were a brand new country. But the coattails of the Civil War were still trailing amongst us and we children were vaguely aware that our neighbours were not all marching to the sound of the same drum. My republican grandmother had different thinking to my father, for example, and even though we children could not decipher the reason we were still aware of it. But while some people were hesitant to air their political views, my grandmother had no such problem. She loved to tell stories of all that had gone on and my one regret now is that we did not spend more time listening to her. She regaled us with stories about the Black and Tans, an auxiliary army of the British forces, who raided her home regularly late at night as she often sheltered local republicans with whom they were waging a guerrilla war. She hid the 'boys on the run', as they were known, and amongst them was a young man whom the Black and Tans were particularly anxious to apprehend – and when a concerned neighbour advised against sheltering this young man as she might get burnt out, he was told: 'We must look after him because his father is dead and his mother is a fool.' As she told me this story I enquired as to the reason for her opinion of the mother, to be informed: 'They were a grand family until his father got married and she ruined a fine family.' No further explanation was forthcoming.

In school we were all marching to the 'nation once again' drum. Our teachers encouraged us to love Ireland, and they taught us many songs and poems that helped grow and develop our love of our native land.

My Land
She is a rich and rare land;
Oh! she's a fresh and fair land
She is a dear and rare land –
This native land of mine.

No men than hers were braver –
Her women's hearts ne'er waver;
I'd freely die to save her,
And think my lot divine.

She's not a dull or cold land;
No! she's a warm and bold land;
Oh! she's a true and old land –
This native land of mine.

Could beauty ever guard her,
And virtue still reward her,
No foe would cross her border –
No friend within it pine.

Oh! She's a fresh and fair land,
Oh! she's a true and rare land;
Yes, she's a rare and fair land –
This native land of mine.

Thomas Davis

These poets sowed the seeds of idealism and love of place in our young minds and on looking along our valley I felt that ours was the countryside they were talking about and I was delighted that we were part of it all. There was a great sense of awareness and appreciation of what was now ours after long years of being under outside domination. They imbued in us a great love of our own country. Intermingled with this patriotism were staunch Catholic beliefs that were darned into our lives in school and reinforced by my mother at home, but my father viewed the over-zealous Church practices of the time with a cryptic cynicism. Every Sunday morning he turned on the BBC and we listened to the Church of England service before going to Mass, and he told us, 'We might be all marching to the sound of different drums, but we are all going in the same direction.' His God was out in the fields and to him the laws of nature were part of the divine plan.

He loved quoting from a poem about King Cormac MacAirt which probably appealed to him because nature intervened and carried out the dead monarch's wishes to be buried with the new religion, Christianity, rather than with paganism. My father's favourite lines were:

> But bury me at Rossnaree
> And face me to the rising sun.

But though Christianity was well entrenched in the country, the dying traces of paganism were still talked about and the practice of pisheogs was well remembered. The pisheogs were a form of curse or black magic that could be wished on a victim by an evil-minded neighbour who wanted to send bad luck their way. This curse could be carried out by placing a harmful token, such as rotten eggs or even a dead animal, on the neighbour's property. It was an evil and scary practice, and sometimes the victim had Mass offered to counteract this demonic intent. So long, long after King Cormac had embraced Christianity traces of paganism were still remembered.

The Burial of King Cormac

King Cormac Mac Airt lived long before Saint Patrick came to Ireland. In those days the people of this country were pagans and worshipped false gods of wood and stone. Yet it is said that Cormac, in his old age, learned in some way of the true God, and no longer worshipped the false gods of his people.

Cormac first heard of the true God at Ross, on the Banks of the Boyne. He gave orders that he was to be buried there when he died, and not at Brugh, farther up the river, where all the kings who went before him were buried.

One day when Cormac was eating a salmon, one of the bones stuck in his throat and choked him. When the Druids, or pagan priests, heard the news they said: 'He has been punished

now for mocking the gods of old. Let us bury him at Brugh
with his father and his father's father.'

But on the day of the funeral, when those who carried the
corpse tried to cross the Boyne to Brugh, the river rose in a
mighty flood and swept the coffin from their shoulders. Next
morning it was found on the bank of the river at Ross, and
there it was buried. So Cormac lies, not in pagan Brugh, but
at Ross where he had first heard of the one true God.

Spread not the beds of Brugh for me
When restless death-bed's use is done:
But bury me at Rossnaree
And face me to the rising sun.

Samuel Ferguson

My father obviously had the same schoolbook as I had and
that story had caught his imagination. We walked through
the same fields going to school as my father and grandfather
had, and probably sat in the same desks because our desks
had the appearance of having endured generations of belting and battering. These desks also were the records of the
names of past pupils, with row upon row of names inscribed
into them. Sometimes the Christian name of one pupil had
inadvertently joined the family name of a neighbour due
to the fact that their own name had been written over by
the next generation of neighbours. These desks were made
to last, with strong iron legs beneath solid oak benches, and
attached oak tops along which were drop-in holes for ink
wells. These desks had the look of having been there since

the time of Adam.

Each desk seated about six or seven depending on class numbers, posterior sizes and availability. Sometimes getting to your place necessitated a hefty bottom-and-shoulder push to facilitate maximum capacity. Ours was a mixed school long before co-ed was heard of, and usually the girls sat together, with the boys opting for the back benches unless one of them was hauled to the front for misdemeanours. Sometimes mini-battles that had begun out in the playground continued inside, between and beneath the desks, until the Master called law and order. Our schoolbooks too were hand-me-downs, with the names of past generations inscribed on them, and sometimes those of neighbouring families. In some ways this gave the sense that we were one big, extended, long-tailed family. We all lived along the same valley where our families had farmed for generations and where the *meitheal* tradition was strong, so not only did we children go to school together but we often came together again with the adults for saving the hay, cutting the corn, threshing, or going to the bog.

Standing on our doorstep you could view the school in the distance across the fields. My mother could see us escaping into the freedom of the big field below the school, and we could look across the valley at our home nestling in the trees. A river curved along this valley and the fields of the farms on the sloping hillsides on either side told the story of the lives of the people living there. The work was done by horses, so the only sounds to be heard were the lowing of the cows, the braying of donkeys, the singing of the birds, or the call of a farmer with good vocal chords shouting a long-distance message across the fields to his neighbour. Other than these occasional sounds it was a valley filled with monastic tranquility.

Chapter 11

Knights of the Road

As well as the stories from ancient Ireland, more recent history and stories entered our lives too, both formally at school and informally around the fire at night. In Ireland we had the tradition of the bards and druids who entertained and soothed people with their music and song. Some of these travelled between the great houses long ago, others were attached to a specific house, while others travelled the roads, staying anywhere and everywhere in welcoming homes along the way. In their time they were the mobile culture of Ireland and were much appreciated by the people to whom their music, song and stories brought rays of light, delight and creativity. Our resilient ancestors appreciated this break in their hard-working routine, and from time to time enjoyed a joyous reunion with these entertaining travellers. Over the years deep friendships were

formed between the performers and their hosts, and particularly with the children to whom their visit was an occasion of total joy. And out of those bonds came ballads like 'Pinch and Caoch O'Leary'.

Our old neighbour, Bill, taught us this ballad when we had our lessons done at night as we sat around the fire toasting our toes before going to bed. In one sense, Bill was our bard and druid, as he taught us many things, including Irish dancing. I well recall learning the 'Fairy Reel', which often dissolved into a tangle of legs and howls of laughter. This annoyed the blazes out of Bill who took Irish dancing skills very seriously. And if anyone cheated at cards he lost the plot altogether! But he got listening ears from very appreciative and willing students for his recital of 'Pinch and Caoch O'Leary'.

This was a very sad story and Bill lowered his voice and became very still as he began, and we all settled down to listen quietly and respectfully because we had heard this poem many times and knew that it was a story of great loss. We mourned for Caoch and his dog Pinch, and felt that it could be the dreaded TB disease, that was rampant in our time, or the famine that had carried away Eily, Kate and Mary. We did not know, but sensed, that they were part of all our past sadnesses. Maybe there is in the soul of Ireland the pain of many losses: loss of land, the Great Hunger, loss of people to emigration and the plague of poverty and other illnesses. So it could be that in listening to the story of Pinch and Caoch we were attending respectfully to the losses of our ancestors down through the centuries and the familiar sound of Bill's voice made it our story too. Children have a great sense of drama and to us this was drama right here in our own kitchen.

Pinch and Caoch O'Leary
One winter's day, long, long ago,
When I was a little fellow
A piper wandered to my door,
Grey-headed, blind and yellow
And oh! how glad was my young heart,
Though earth and sky looked dreary,
To see the stranger and his dog –
Poor Pinch and Caoch O'Leary.

And when he stowed away his 'bag',
Cross-barred with green and yellow
I thought and said 'In Ireland's ground
There's not so fine a fellow.'
And then he stroked my flaxen hair,
And cried, 'God mark my deary!'
And how I wept when he said 'Farewell',
And thought of Caoch O'Leary!

Well, twenty summers had gone past,
And June's red sun was sinking,
When I, a man sat by my door,
Of twenty sad things thinking.

A little dog came up the way,
His gait was slow and weary,
And at his tail a lame man limped –
'Twas Pinch and Caoch O'Leary!

'God's blessing here!' the wanderer cried,
'Far, far be hell's black viper;
Does anybody hereabouts
Remember Caoch the Piper?'
With swelling heart I grasped his hand;
The old man murmured, 'Deary,
Are you the silky-headed child
That loved poor Caoch O'Leary?'

'Yes, yes,' I said – the wanderer wept
As if his heart was breaking –
'And where, a vic machree,' he sobbed,
'Is all the merry-making
I found here twenty years ago?'
'My tale,' I sighed, 'might weary;
Enough to say – there's none but me
To welcome Caoch O'Leary.'

'Vo, vo, vo,' the old man cried
And wrung his hands in sorrow,
'Pray let me in, astore machree
And I'll go home tomorrow.
My peace is made; I'll gladly leave

This world so cold and dreary
And you shall keep my pipes and dog,
And pray for Caoch O'Leary.'

With Pinch I watched his bed that night;
Next day his wish was granted;
He died; and Father John was brought
And Requiem Mass was chanted.
The neighbours came; we dug his grave
Near Eily, Kate and Mary,
And there he sleeps his last sweet sleep:
God rest you! Caoch O'Leary.

John Keegan

This long, narrative poem was folk memory and history all rolled into one, and with the capacity of children to listen to the same story over and over again we never grew tired of listening to Bill recite the poem of Pinch and Caoch O'Leary.

But 'An Old Woman of the Roads', which was in everybody's schoolbook, tells another story. It paints such a graphic picture of a deep desire and longing for a home, it's easy to identify with it. We all want the security of our own home.

An Old Woman of the Roads
Oh, to have a little house!
To own the hearth and stool and all!

The heaped-up sods upon the fire,
The pile of turf against the wall!

To have a clock with weights and chains,
And pendulum swinging up and down!
A dresser filled with shining delph,
Speckled and white and blue and brown!

I could be busy all the day
Clearing and sweeping hearth and floor,
And fixing on their shelf again
My white and blue and speckled store!

I could be quiet there at night
Beside the fire and by myself,
Sure of a bed and loth to leave
The ticking clock and shining delph!

Och! but I'm weary of mist and dark,
And roads where there's never a house nor bush,
And tired I am of bog and road,
And the crying wind and the lonesome hush!

And I am praying to God on high,
And I am praying Him night and day,
For a little house – a house of my own –
Out of the wind's and the rain's way.

Padraic Colum

There is a deep sadness in this poem and I can remember feeling an ache of loneliness for the old woman as she trudged the roads in despair. Ours was the era of the Travelling People and when they came to our area they camped by the bridge at the bottom of the hill below our house. They came in colourful horse-drawn caravans, though some of them just had carts and at night would set up their canvas camps under the cart. Sometimes during the night they opened the gate into adjoining farm fields to give their horses free grazing, which did not endear them to some farmers, but others had no objections. Also, it was not unknown that they might occasionally help themselves to eggs, chickens or hens. The men were tinsmiths who would repair pots and pans and broken umbrellas, and they also swept chimneys, so they provided a much-needed service at the time. They also traded in horses, and large crowds of them gathered for the local horse fair in our town, and as long hours of drinking were part of these fairs that could sometimes finish up in drunken brawls either between themselves or with members of the local community, and the local guards often came to restore law and order. But both communities got on fairly well together and over the years each side forged working relationships with certain others, and they respected and trusted each other. The travelling women did likewise with rural women, and they brought a certain amount of colour into the lives of these women, as often they were fortune-tellers and they also came with baskets of colourful paper flowers, holy pictures, statues, medals, clothes pegs, mothballs, and endless supplies of other bits and pieces. Of course, we children loved them and to us they were exotic and colourful with their brightly coloured shawls framing tanned faces, from beneath which a brown baby might peep out. We thought that they had a great life on the road, a colourful life full of activity, a wonderful life and we envied them. So the following poem painted a perfect picture of what we visualised their life on the road to be. Children always want happy endings! Don't we all?

The Pedlar's Caravan
I wish I lived in a caravan,
With a horse to drive, like a pedlar-man!
Where he comes from nobody knows,
Or where he goes to, but on he goes.

His caravan has windows two,
And a chimney of tin, that the smoke comes through;
He has a wife, with a baby brown,
And they go riding from town to town.

Chairs to mend, and delf to sell!
He clashes the basins like a bell;
Tea-trays, baskets ranged in order,
Plates with the alphabet round the border.

The roads are brown, and the sea is green,
But his house is like a bathing machine;

The world is round, and he can ride,
Rumble and splash to the other side.

With the pedlar-man I should like to roam,
And write a book when I came home;
All the people would read my book,
Just like the Travels of Captain Cook.

W. B. Rands

There was a different kind of traveller poem in our school-books too, a kind of wanderer-dreamer poem, where we imagine another life, elsewhere. These we studied more at secondary-school level. I well remember our English teacher – she and her husband had set up a small secondary school in our town. She was quick-tempered, impatient and intolerant, and to our minds certainly not designed for teaching! But she had one overriding virtue in that she loved English literature with a passion, and she managed to impart this to us. She wanted desperately to get into our minds the images that the writers painted in hers and she must have suffered greatly trying to transplant the complexities of Hopkins and the intricacies of Shakespearean language into our disinterested heads. She tried very hard to encourage in us an appreciation of Yeats and explained his dream world, as expressed in this poem that everybody in Ireland will have learned at some stage.

The Lake Isle of Innisfree

I will arise and go now, and go to Innisfree,

And a small cabin build there, of clay and wattles made;

Nine bean-rows will I have there, a hive for the honey-
bee,

And live alone in the bee-loud glade.

And I shall have some peace there, for peace comes
dropping slow,

Dropping from the veils of the morning to where the
cricket sings;

There midnight's all a-glimmer, and noon a purple
glow,

And evening full of the linnet's wings.

I will arise and go now, for always night and day

I hear lake water lapping with low sounds by the shore;

While I stand on the roadway, or on the pavements
grey,

I hear it in the deep heart's core.

W.B. Yeats

The travelling woman of 'An Old Woman of the Roads' and
the poet W.B. Yeats were from two different worlds, but both
dreamed of another place. I wonder if this fostered a wan-
derlust in us too? The poets and writers in our schoolbooks
took us on many an imaginary and enjoyable journey, and
the words and the imagery stayed forever printed on the

back pages of our minds.

In 'The Song of Wandering Aengus', Yeats created a vision of a visit into a fantasy world which opened doors in our minds that enabled us to extend our world into that zone. If a poet could create these worlds why not we as well? Children know no boundaries of the imagination. On a distant hill across the river from our house was a long, meandering wood known as the Island Wood, and as I learned 'The Song of Wandering Aengus' that became *my* hazel wood. We seldom visited it because it was so far away over many fields and we had to cross the river *en route*, but when we went there at Christmas to collect holly it was a dark, mysterious place full of glistening green holly. Maybe the fact that it was far away and somewhat unattainable added to its mystical appeal.

The Song of Wandering Aengus
I went out to the hazel wood,
Because a fire was in my head,
And cut and peeled a hazel wand,
And hooked a berry to a thread;
And when white moths were on the wing,
And moth-like stars were flickering out,
I dropped the berry in a stream
And caught a little silver trout.

When I had laid it on the floor
I went to blow the fire a-flame,
But something rustled on the floor,
And someone called me by my name:
It had become a glimmering girl
With apple blossom in her hair
Who called me by my name and ran
And faded through the brightening air.

Though I am old with wandering
Through hollow lands and hilly lands,
I will find out where she has gone,
And kiss her lips and take her hands;
And walk among long dappled grass,
And pluck till time and times are done,
The silver apples of the moon,
The golden apples of the sun.

W.B. Yeats

And now on the road between Innishannon and Bandon we have a sculpture of 'The Song of Wandering Aengus' – not an easy poem to depict in stone, but this beautiful sculpture captures the indefinable imagery and magic of the poem.

Chapter 12

The Long Memory

In our secondary-school years, poems were parsed and analysed, but when we were in the junior classes with no such requirements, the essence and rhythms of the words simply soaked into our senses and we took our own meaning and our own sense of rhythm from them. 'The Minstrel Boy' was up for grabs and we decided that this was a marching song with a military beat, so we marched around the kitchen in military formation, cracking our strong leather boots with their iron-tipped heels off the stone floor and singing it at the tops of our voices. This was to help us learn off the words because we must have thought that the rhythm of the steps would beat the words more easily into our brains. Our long-suffering mother never protested!

Niall Naoigiallac

b'é cuacal ceaccmar ...
clocan árd ríogacais nuair a zab s...
Socur cormac Mac Airc céim eile cuz...
sé ceampair. Ac be **Niall Naoigiallac** ...
cur an t-árd-ríogacas ar a bonnaib iz ceart...
ar Connaccaib agus coimnuide air, breacmair cu...
400 aд. Cuaid cruir da' clauny mac o cuaid gur...
eids bí fágca de sean-cuize Ullad. Eogan, Co...
na dob' ainm doib agus haimmnigead uaca na cal...
— Cír Cogain, **Cír Connaill** agus **Cír Caona** . Ci' d...
arb ainm do brion agus gab seiscann calcai san...
m, agus i **Roscomain** . Ci' driocaireaca eile a...
Nuigeo agus i **Sligeac** , agus bi' clauny mac age a...
'r na cire, **Sloic Néill** a cuzai' ina diaid sin...
m a bi i zceannas i ndún na ngall agus ...
Mide , larmide , Cilldara , longpoz...

The Minstrel Boy

The Minstrel Boy to the war is gone,
In the ranks of death you'll find him;
His father's sword he has girded on,
And his wild harp slung behind him.
'Land of song!' said the warrior-bard,
'Though all the world betrays thee,
One sword, at least, thy rights shall guard,
One faithful harp shall praise thee!'

The Minstrel fell!– but the foeman's chain
Could not bring his proud soul under;
The harp he loved ne'er spoke again,
For he tore its chords asunder;
And said, 'No chains shall sully thee,
Thou soul of love and bravery!
Thy songs were made for the pure and free,
They shall never sound in slavery.'

Thomas Moore

Some of these poems and stories stayed with us, or at least bits of them did, never to be forgotten. It's probably the lines that we loved most that we best remember. When my father quoted his favourite lines you could feel that he enjoyed remembering them because his face assumed a different expression and his voice changed, and you knew that he was visualising the scene he was describing. Years afterwards I could not differentiate whether it was he or I who had originally learnt the following poem, so maybe the two of us had learnt it and shared the pleasure of remembering it together. When my father quoted from it he did so in deep, sombre tones as if he was delivering a eulogy at a funeral. Maybe he felt that he should in some way be in harmony with what he was reciting.

The Harp that Once through Tara's Halls
The harp that once through Tara's halls
The soul of music shed,
Now hangs as mute on Tara's walls,
As if that soul were fled.
So sleeps the pride of former days,
So glory's thrill is oe'r,
And hearts, that once beat high for praise,
Now feel that pulse no more.

No more to chiefs and ladies bright
The harp of Tara swells,
The chord alone that breaks at night,
Its tale of ruin tells.
Thus freedom now so seldom wakes,
The only throb she gives,
Is when some heart indignant breaks,
To show that still she lives.

Thomas Moore

Whereas 'The Minstrel Boy' had an invigorating tempo and beat, and the memories of 'Tara's Halls' spoke of faded glories of the past, there was another poem more finely tuned in its pathos and we learned this with a sense of sadness because the poet captured an almost intangible essence into which we were drawn. The 'Lament for Thomas McDonagh' has a deep sense of loss delicately interwoven into the fields, so we could identify with the scene that Francis Ledwidge was painting. The lowing of a cow is a deep, earthy, mournful sound – maybe the bellowing in the pain of calving echoes the pathos and depth of the poem. We knew all about the delight of the cows in 'pleasant meads' as we saw it regularly when they sighted fresh fields of grazing, so despite the sadness of the poem we got the ray of hope at the very end. Francis Ledwidge was speaking our language.

Lament for Thomas McDonagh
He shall not hear the bittern cry
In the wild sky where he is lain,
Nor voices of the sweeter birds,
Above the wailing of the rain.

Nor shall he know when loud March blows
Thro' slanting snows her fanfare shrill,
Blowing to flame the golden cup
Of many an upset daffodil.

But when the Dark Cow leaves the moor
And pastures poor with greedy weeds
Perhaps he'll hear her low at morn,
Lifting her horn in pleasant meads.

Francis Ledwidge

The poems of our poets were part of us and gave voice to our thoughts, and enabled us to see our world through their eyes. What a gift! As he grew old my father would sometimes smilingly quote his favourite bit from Thomas Moore's song 'Oft in the Stilly Night', a great favourite with his generation.

...I feel like one
Who treads alone
Some banquet-hall deserted,
Whose lights are fled,
Whose garlands dead,
And all but he departed!

But he was not a singer, and on the night of the Stations or the threshing, or when there was a family gathering for returned emigrants and there was a sing-song, my father opted out. But the rest of us waded in whether we were talented or otherwise. My brother was our lead singer as he had a wonderful tenor voice and could soar high with 'The Lark in the Clear Air' or slow down to 'She Moved through the Fair'. All my sisters were good singers and so we ranged from the foot of 'Sliabh na mBan' to where the 'Shannon River Meets the Sea'. Eventually the self-appointed compere for the night would look in my direction, but unfortunately I was not vocally blessed and the sister who was in charge of operations was delighted to introduce me as the crow of the family. But the audience were kind and helpful, and would helicopter in with a rescue remedy when I faltered, and a combined chorus would help me get Kate and Pat McGee from 'Way Down in the County Kerry' jigging into action around the kitchen floor. When the repertoire of the young was eventually exhausted it was the turn of some of neighbours, and the party piece of one man was 'Emmet's Speech from the Dock', to which we all listened with rapt attention. This particular neighbour had only one string to his party bow and because we heard it at every sing-song we could all repeat it word-perfect, so if Emmet lost his direction around the dock we soon had him upright and back in full flow. Recitations were very much part of any gathering and 'The Shooting of Dan McGrew' and 'The Road Downhill was an Easy Road, so that was the road we went' were all familiar to our ears. Maybe because emigration was very much part of our lives, some of the recitations had an American cowboy flavour. Then Mick, who lived nearby, always had his 'box' at the ready and so the songs and recitations were often interspersed with instrumental recitals with which we could sometimes sing along. My mother was not into singing but would eventually be persuaded to comply and would come forth with:

Darling, I am growing old,
Silver threads among the gold.

She had another song that I have never heard sung since and
I now remember only the first few lines (I tried Google and
it failed me! First time for everything.).

In a tumble-down attic,
That was grim and bare,
An old man lay dying one day,
He said he was dying
But clasped in his hand
Was a letter that was faded and grey.

And the song continued on to tell a sad saga of a long-
forgotten love affair where his beloved married his best
friend, with all the usual romantic remembering. We thought
that it was wonderful because, of course, little girls can never
get enough romantic stories, especially ones about lost loves.
So my poor mother had to make regular visits up to this
tumble-down attic. She must often have regretted taking us
up there in the first place!

But mingled through all these songs, poems, myths, legends and facts, came a strong sense of our roots.

Chapter 13

Royal Roots

For children, abandonment by their parents must be the most heart-breaking and unimaginable fate possible, and for that reason the story of the Children of Lir lingers forever in a child's memory. So the fate that befell the Children of Lir was for us terrifying and the fact that it happened thousands of years earlier made no difference because children have no concept of that kind of time span. This myth connected us to our ancient roots of Irishness. In my childhood we were a new nation, but were still well rooted back in an ancient past of old stories and legends.

The voices of the Children of Lir have never faded for me. They echo down through the corridors of our history and can still be heard in our music and song. We celebrate them too in many images, children's stories and Celtic designs.

This is the version I remember best. We learned it in one of the senior classes at primary school from the Land of Youth readers.

The Children of Lir

Silent; oh Moyle!, be the roar of thy waters,
Break not, ye breezes, your chains of repose,
While, murmuring mournfully, Lir's lonely daughter,
Tells to the night-star her tale of woes.

When shall the swan, her death-note ringing,
Sleep, with wings in darkness furl'd?
When will heav'n, its sweet bell ringing,
Call my spirit from this stormy world?

Sadly, oh Moyle, to thy winter wave weeping,
Fate bids me languish long ages away,
Yet still in her darkness doth Erin lie sleeping,
Still doth the pure light its dawning delay.

When will that day-star, mildly springing,
Warm our isle with peace and love?
When will heav'n, its sweet bell ringing,
Call my spirit to the fields above.

Thomas Moore

In this poem Thomas Moore blends together the legend of the Children of Lir and the story of the first bells of Christianity pealing in Erin. The legend of the Children of Lir tells us about King Lir and his four much-loved, beautiful children, Fionnuala, Aodh, Fiachra and Conn, who had been turned into four swans by their jealous step-mother for nine hundred years. The heartbroken father spent the remainder of his life at the side of Lake Derravarragh to be near his children. Under the spell the children retained their human voices and could still sing beautifully, which was a great source of comfort to their father. People who came to the lakeside were soothed and calmed by their wonderful singing. Their first three hundred years were spent in that lake, the second three hundred years in the Sea of Moyle, and the third three hundred years in Sidh Fionnachaidh. The wicked spell would be broken only when they would hear the first bell of Christianity toll. When they heard the bell, the spell was broken and they came out of the lake but were immediately changed into very, very old people, who lay down and died. But before they died, the monk Caomhog christened them, and as they died the children changed back into the beautiful children they had been nine hundred years earlier.

This legend has interwoven its mystical essence into our minds – when we see beautiful swans floating on a calm lake they stir strands of that story. The story also comes alive when we watch the beautiful ballet *Swan Lake*, and the legend adds to its pathos. Myths and legends have the uncanny knack of darning themselves into the fabric of our memories and weaving a special magic that is never quite forgotten. Even when we have gone past the age of swallowing tall tales, they still retain the mystery of the unknown and a flavour of the children we once were, who never doubted their reality.

Stories of Fionn MacCumhail and the Fianna were also sprinkled through our schoolbooks. They were held up as heroes and we never analysed if they were real historical figures or otherwise. They were great stories and we swallowed them with unquestioning appreciation. This following story comes from a tattered schoolbook with my name on the cover. It could have been the third- or fourth-class book, and I would have been about ten years old when I learned it.

Fionn MacCumhail and His Friends

The Fianna of Erin were a famous band of heroes, many hundreds of years ago, in the days when the great Cormac was king. They were foot-soldiers, armed with sword and spear and shield. Some of them were the king's body-guard, while others kept watch round the coast to see that no enemy landed.

Their principal camp was on the hill of Allen in Kildare. When not on duty they occupied their time in hunting and fishing. They were strong men, very tall and broad, and were chosen for their courage, skill, and endurance. They were bound by strict vows not only to be brave in battle, but also to be kind and gentle and to speak the truth.

Fionn MacCumhail was their great captain, and about him and his friends many stories are told, in some of which he is pictured as a man of magic powers and of giant size. He was said to have tasted of the Salmon of Knowledge and to be able to see into the future. He had also a marvellous horn which could be heard all over the country, and one note from it summoned all the heroes together to the camp of their chief.

Among Fionn's faithful friends was his dog, Bran. She was a fierce, small-headed, white-breasted hound. The old bards tell us that she had the eyes of a dragon, the claws of a wolf and the strength of a lion. She must have been a splendid creature, and Fionn had good reason to be proud of her.

When Fionn's horn sounded a call to battle, Bran understood, and would wail and mourn until her master returned in safety. But there was another note of the horn which above all the things in the world she loved most. This was a call to the chase. In the chase she led all the other hounds, just as her master led all the heroes to battle. She was so sharp and intelligent that people said that she, too, possessed Fionn's gift of knowledge.

Many places in Ireland remind us of Fionn. When we see the outline of the Sleeping Giant on the Cave Hill in Belfast, or the curiously-shaped rocks of the Giant's Causeway in Antrim, or the huge stones on top of so many of our Irish mountains, or the wide deep clefts in our cliffs – these all speak to us of the hero.

He is said to have slept in the great cave on the Cave Hill, and to have built the Giant's Causeway so that he and his men might step across from Ireland to Scotland. One of the big clefts is called Fionn's Leap, because he could jump so lightly across it. And as for the big stones, the heroes are said to have hurled them from hill-top to hill-top out of sport.

Marie Bayne

Was it any wonder that we thought of Fionn as a super-hero? He was the pop star of our time and because he was long gone there was no possibility of anything denting his image, and we could visualise him in any format that we fancied.

St Patrick also featured big in our childhood and even though we were not quite sure what the conflict between paganism and Christianity that was often mentioned in our schoolbooks was all about, the concept of going from dark-ness into light got the message across fairly well. But to us, St Patrick's greatest claim to fame was that he evicted the snakes out of Ireland. That was his most remarkable achieve-ment, as far as we were concerned.

St Patrick's Day was a great occasion and for days before-hand we went out searching for shamrock along the ditches – and if you came home with a bunch of clover you were immediately rescheduled to go forth and try again. It was a great scoop to find a big, draping cluster of shamrock to cascade down the front of your lapel. Bunches of sham-rock were posted to many parts of the world, but mainly to America where St Patrick's Day was a big event. There were special cardboard boxes decorated on the outside with shamrock for posting. Later, St Patrick's Day badges came on board and these replaced or sometimes embellished the display of shamrocks on the frontage. We children competed with each other as to how greener-than-green we could look on St Patrick's Day. But at the age of about twelve I went out in the local parade dressed as St Patrick, wearing a long floating pink (not green!) taffeta dress (courtesy of a bridesmaid from a neighbour's wedding), bearing a silver crown cobbled together in cardboard and covered in silver paper by a sister, and carrying a glass walking stick courtesy of a returned Yank. I had on a pair of fake leather crocodile slippers, and where they came from I have now no idea, but certainly not from my mother who would not have been seen dead in a pair of them. I must have looked a fair sight, but thought that I was the bee's knees, and St Patrick must have been cringing on high at his colourful taudry depiction.

We loved the way he set up his fire before the pagan king got around to lighting his. To us it took great guts to take on the king because in our world you complied with regulations, and his rebel action appealed to us because in school, or indeed at home, rebelliousness was not tolerated.

The Paschal Fire of Patrick
On Tara's hill the daylight dies,
On Tara's plain 'tis dead.
'Till Baal's enkindled fires shall rise
No fire must flame instead.'
'Tis thus the King commanding speaks,
For lo! a fire defiant breaks
From out the woods of Slane.

For there in prayer is Patrick bent,
With Christ his soul is knit;
And there before his simple tent
The Paschal fire is lit.
'What means this flame that through the night
Illumines all the vale?
What rebel hand a fire dare light
Before the fires of Baal?'

O King! when Baal's dark reign is o'er,
When thou thyself art gone,
This fire will light the Irish shore
And lead its people on;
Will lead them on full many a night
Through which they're doomed to go,
Like that which led the Israelite
From bondage and from woe.

This fire, this sacred fire of God,
Young hearts shall bear afar
To lands no human foot hath trod
Beneath the western star;
To lands where Faith's bright flag unfurled
By those who here have knelt
Shall give unto a newer world
The sceptre of the Celt.

D.F. Mc Carthy

To us paganism was part of the past and Christianity was the bright new thinking. A wave of religious zeal was flowing through the country that was intent on asserting its new political and religious independence. We loved all the trappings that came with the annual Mission to our local church, though most of what the missionaries said went over our heads. We could not get enough holy pictures and statues with which to adorn the house and, of course, the May altar gave us another opportunity to go on a real rampage of statues and flowers. Our lady was the top favourite with St Thérèse coming a close second, and the belief that St Thérèse could send down a shower of roses when requested was the stuff that dreams were made of. The Corpus Christi procession that paraded all around the town in June, with beautifully robed clergy and rows of the faithful bearing colourful confraternity banners, and decorations with flags and bunting flying along the way, and windows and doorways of houses full of flowers and statues all made for a great day as far as we children were concerned.

Chapter 14

Through the Eyes of a Child

Some people never lose their inner child. One such person was Robert Louis Stevenson, who constantly wove magic into the world of our childhood. His was the well-heeled world of nurseries and nannies and very far removed from our life of running across fields to school. He was a delicate child plagued by ill health, and yet he had the writing skill to cross all these barriers and unite our different worlds. Such was his ability to draw us into his world that even though he was writing about situations that were completely unknown to us he could still make us feel part of it all. Even as an adult he never lost the playful mind of a child and could fill our world with his sense of fun. In this poem he introduced us to our shadows and showed us what fun we could have with them.

My Shadow

I have a little shadow that goes in and out with me,
And what can be the use of him is more than I can see.
He is very, very like me from the heels up to the head;
And I see him jump before me, when I jump into bed.

The funniest thing about him is the way he likes to
    grow –
Not at all like proper children, which is always very
    slow;
For he sometimes shoots up taller like an india-rubber
    ball,
And he sometimes gets so little that there's none of
    him at all.

He hasn't got a notion of how children ought to play,
And can only make a fool of me in every sort of way.
He stays so close beside me, he's a coward, you can see;
I'd think shame to stick to nursie as that shadow sticks
    to me!

One morning, very early, before the sun was up,
I rose and found the shining dew on every buttercup;
But my lazy little shadow, like an arrant sleepy-head,
Had stayed at home behind me and was fast asleep in
    bed.

R.L. Stevenson

168

We had never thought about our shadows before but now they became objects of great fascination. We looked out for the effect the light had on our shadows at different times of the day. Coming home from school we watched them move along with us, and we sometimes danced to simply watch our shadows do the same thing. It was almost as if our shadows were separate from us but imitating us instead of being part of us. If you were alone, it could become a playmate and you could have a lot of fun dancing with your shadow. Sometimes we created animal heads on the walls with our hands and fingers and tried to out-do each other with the skilful shaping and manoeuvring our shadow figures. We even played imaginary games along the walls if sent to bed early on a summer evening.

Then there was a lesson in one of our schoolbooks that told us more about the writer who had written this amazing poem with which we were having such fun.

A Beloved Writer

It was natural that Robert Louis Stevenson should write a great deal about travel, for he was a traveller nearly all his life. As a child he took imaginary journeys in his home in Edinburgh, enjoying all sorts of fanciful adventures while he lay in bed or played about the garden. He was often ill, and not strong enough to play rough games. When he felt lonely he used to say to himself:

The world is so great, and I am so small,
I do not like it at all, at all.

But after a while he changed this saying to another:

The world is so full of a number of things
I'm sure we should all be as happy as kings.

… From one place to another Stevenson was taken to
improve his health. When he grew up he spent a great deal
of his time in France. One of his most interesting journeys
was in the south of France, in the company of a little donkey,
which carried his food and his sleeping-sack. The book in
which his adventures on this trip are described is called *Travels
with a Donkey*.

He wrote another travel-book about a journey in a canoe,
partly in France and partly in Belgium. Two of his journeys
took him to America, the first time to California, and the
second time to the Adirondack Mountains, in the state of
New York, where he hoped to find good health.

Stevenson was tall and thin, his brown eyes were large and
very bright, and all his movements were graceful. Although he
was dogged by ill-health, no one was ever more cheerful and
gay, or enjoyed life more. He was kindly and sympathetic, and
could talk delightfully, so he made countless friends.

He was a tireless worker. When he was so ill that he could
not read or even speak aloud, he wrote some of the poems
in *A Child's Garden of Verses*. Besides poems and books of
travel, he wrote many stories, long and short. One of the most
popular is *Treasure Island*, a pirate story full of adventure, written for boys but enjoyed by girls too.

Of all his journeys the longest was to the South Sea, where
for more than three years he sailed about from one beauti-

ful island to another. At last he decided to make his home in those parts and he built a house on a mountainside in Samoa, where the weather is always warm, and the birds sing and the flowers blossom all the year round. Yet even in this earthly paradise, where he found happiness and enjoyed a fuller measure of health than he had known, his thoughts often went back to Scotland and to his wind-swept, inclement native city.

He died in Samoa in 1894, only forty-six years old, and he was buried on the top of the mountain by the dark-skinned natives who loved him. Carved on his headstone are the three last lines for his own Requiem:

Under the wide and starry sky
Dig the grave and let me lie.
Glad did I live and gladly die,
And I laid me down with a will.

This be the verse you grave for me:
Here he lies where he longed to be;
Home is the sailor, home from sea,
And the hunter home from the hill.

This was my first brush with biography and travel writing. It amazed me that one individual could lead such an interesting and varied life. How wonderful it seemed to travel to such faraway and unusual places. Such was Stevenson's ability to make what he was writing about feel like our world that we never really considered him as writing about a different place. He travelled with us through our childhood and what a wonderful companion he was. That lesson in our schoolbook led us to seek out his book *Treasure Island* in the small local County Council library that had just opened in our town. Then a poem from Stevenson's book *A Child's Garden of Verses* later appeared in another schoolbook.

Escape at Bedtime

The lights from the parlour and kitchen shone out
Through the blinds and the windows and bars;
And high overhead and all moving about,
There were thousands of millions of stars.
There ne'er were such thousands of leaves on a tree,
Nor of people in church or the Park,
As the crowds of the stars that looked down upon me,
And that glittered and winked in the dark.

The Dog, and the Plough, and the Hunter, and all,
And the star of the sailor, and Mars,
These shone in the sky, and the pail by the wall
Would be half full of water and stars.
They saw me at last, and they chased me with cries,
And they soon had me packed into bed;
But the glory kept shining and bright in my eyes,
And the stars going round in my head.

R.L. Stevenson

His fascination with the stars and the night sky deepened my interest in them too. Each night, but especially in the summer when an accurate forecast of the weather was vital for successful harvesting, my father stood on the doorstep to read the night sky in order to ascertain from prevailing celestial conditions the weather forecast for the following day. He would already have listened to the forecast on the radio, but had more faith in his own forecasting skills to give him a clearer picture of what was to come and thus enable him to plan his work schedule for the following day. We all knew the rhyme:

A red sky at night
Is a farmer's delight
And a red sky in the morning
Is a shepherd's warning.

Sometimes we joined him on the doorstep and he introduced us to the Plough, the Milky Way and the Northern star.

But to us the main attraction of the night sky was the moon and we were convinced that away up there lived the 'man in the moon' and we were absolutely intrigued by him. There was no doubt in our minds that he existed and we kept a constant eye on him, and he on us! At that time in rural Ireland the embellishment of curtains had yet to adorn farmhouse windows, so in bed at night we could still gaze up at our friend in the moon until we fell asleep. So we were delighted with Stevenson's poem about the moon.

The Moon

The moon has a face like the clock in the hall;
She shines on thieves on the garden wall,
On streets and fields and harbour quays,
And birdies asleep in the forks of the trees.

The squalling cat and the squeaking mouse,
The howling dog by the door of the house,
The bat that lies in bed at noon,
All love to be out by the light of the moon.

But all of the things that belong to the day
Cuddle to sleep to be out of her way;
And flowers and children close their eyes
Till up in the morning the sun shall rise.

R.L. Stevenson

Chapter 15

Surrounded by Water

I n Ireland we are never too far from the sea to which we are connected by so many great rivers, into which run our countless smaller rivers, *glaishes* or streams. In the valley at the bottom of our farm was a winding river known as the Abha Caol (narrow river) into which all the *glaishes* of our farm found their way. Up this river every year from the sea came salmon to spawn in its quiet waters and here also came eels from the Sargasso Sea. As children we swam in that river, but were very aware of the eels from whom we kept a wary distance as we believed they had reversed teeth which they could use viciously on unwelcome intruders into their waters. The eels hovered in a deep, dark pool under a high shadowy bank and we gave this pool a wide berth and played in a much more open section upstream, which was sunnier and shallower. In late summer, when the hay

was saved and before the harvesting of the wheat and barley began, we were taken to Ballybunion for a short holiday. It was the highlight of our year and we were completely over-whelmed by the magnificence of the sea, the towering grey cliffs and the dark deep caves into which the incoming tide thundered. If a ship appeared on the far horizon we sat on the strand watching in awe its progress on the skyline where it appeared to be travelling along the edge of the world. No wonder poems and stories about the sea appealed to us, and there were plenty of them in our schoolbooks.

Sea Fever

I must go down to the seas again, to the lonely sea and
    the sky,
And all I ask is a tall ship and a star to steer her by,
And the wheel's kick and the wind's song and the
    white sail's shaking,
And a grey mist on the sea's face and a grey dawn
    breaking.

I must go down to the seas again, for the call of the
    running tide
Is a wild call and a clear call that may not be denied;
And all I ask is a windy day and the white clouds
    flying,
And the flung spray and the blown spume, and the sea
    gulls crying.

I must go down to the seas again to the vagrant gypsy
life,
To the gull's way and the whale's way were the wind's
like a whetted knife;
And all I ask is a merry yarn from a laughing fellow
rover,
And quiet sleep and a sweet dream when the long
trick's over.

John Masefield

This next one was Con's favourite poem. Many of the poems and lessons in this book have come from his old schoolbooks which he brought from his home in Islandave and arranged around his bedroom. He was a book lover, so his books soon overflowed out of his room and all around the house. After his untimely death from cancer, his books were stored up in the attic. One summer while all was still well he went on a long sailing holiday and came home bronzed and excited about the delights of the sea. He loved the sea and often on a visit to nearby Garretstown when walking along the beach would recite this favourite poem. Now, whenever I walk by the sea the words of this poem by Alfred Lord Tennyson also flood into my mind.

Break, Break, Break
Break, break, break
On thy cold grey stones, O Sea!
And I would that my tongue could utter

The thoughts that arise in me.

O well for the fisherman's boy,
That he shouts with his sister at play!
O well for the sailor lad,
That he sings in his boat on the bay!

And the stately ships go on
To their haven under the hill;
But O for the touch of a vanished hand,
And the sound of a voice that is still!

Break, break, break,
At the foot of thy crags, O Sea!
But the tender grace of a day that is dead
Will never come back to me.

Lord Tennyson

But as well as poems there were prose lessons too and they
filled in the bigger picture, especially of the land of Ireland
beyond our boundaries. The following lesson from the *Land
of Youth Readers* written by Katharine Tynan extended our
horizons. We found this hugely interesting because we had
so many streams flowing through our land and were very
familiar with every inch of them and with the wildlife they
supported, and it was wonderful to link them to the great
rivers of Ireland as Katharine Tynan does here – it made us
feel part of a bigger picture.

Ireland of the Streams

She is the greenest country ever was seen. I think of the fat
pasture lands at the gates of Dublin, as well I know them. In
May they are drifts of greenness, with the cattle sunken to
their knees. The meadows, white with daisies, gold with but-
tercups, are exceedingly bright and clean. Grass-green, milk-
white, pure gold – these are fields of delight.

I think of the lavish Irish hedges and of the strip of grass
white with daisies which runs along either side of the foot-
path. There is nearly always a clear stream running along the
ditch. It has come down from the mountains, and is amber-
brown in colour. It runs over pebbles that are pure gold and
silver and precious stones, now and again getting dammed
around a boulder, making a leap to escape, and coming
around the boulder with a swirl and a few specks of foam
floating upon it.

'Ireland of the Streams' is one of the old names for Ireland,
and it is justified; for not only are there lordly rivers like the
Shannon and the Blackwater, to mention but two of them,
but there are innumerable little streams everywhere.

You can always kneel down on a summer's day by one, cup
your two hands, and drink your fill. You may track it, if you
will, up to the mountains, where you will find it welling out,
perhaps, through the fronds of a fern, the first tiny gush of it.
You will find it widening out and almost hidden by a mil-
lion flowers and plants that like to stand with their feet in
water. Or you will see it cool and deep, with golden shadows
sleeping in it, slipping round little boulders and clattering
over stones, in a tremendous hurry to escape from these sweet
places to the city, where it will find its way to the sea.

Where there are not rocks and stones and mountains, where there is cultivation in Ireland, there is leafage and grass of great luxuriousness. Of a wet summer in Ireland you could scarcely walk through the grass; it might meet above a child's head.

I do not think the birds are as many as in England, perhaps because so much of Ireland is stripped of its woods; perhaps because Ireland has been slower to protect the birds; perhaps also because of the scantier population, which leaves the birds to suffer hunger in the winter. There are no nightingales in Ireland, but I do not think we have missed them, having the thrush and the blackbird, which seem to me to sing with a richer sweetness in Ireland that in England.

But the most characteristic note of the Irish summer is the corn-crake's. Somehow the Irish corn-crake has a bigger note and is much more in evidence than his English brother.

Katharine Tynan

Now, many years later, as we read about the Dublin of Katharine Tynan's time it comes as a bit of a shock to realise how much has changed in and around Dublin as well as in rural Ireland. On first meeting Gay Byrne in 1988 to be interviewed about my book *To School through the Fields*, I remarked that I had thought he might not get what it was all about, and he replied: 'Dublin has changed as well, you know. I grew up not far from green fields.' And that was right in the city near the South Circular Road! And Katharine Tynan, who was born in Dublin in 1859, had obviously grown up in a still greener Dublin.

Change is constant and when you stand on the bank of a
river or stream the thought comes to mind that they are so
timeless while we are so transient.

The Brook
I chatter, chatter, as I flow
To join the brimming river,
For men may come and men may go,
But I go on for ever.

I wind about, and in and out,
With here a blossom sailing,
And here and there a lusty trout,
And here and there a grayling,

And here and there a foamy flake
Upon me, as I travel
With many a silvery waterbreak
Above the golden gravel,

And draw them all along, and flow
To join the brimming river,
For men may come and men may go,
But I go on for ever.

Lord Tennyson

Chapter 16

Love of Place

One of the treasures I found in the attic was a collection of the work of Oliver Goldsmith. It had once been a beautiful leather-bound edition with its cover embossed in gold, but though it has now lost some of its lustre, it is still a gorgeous book. Old books never lose their elegance and maybe the years of use add to their appeal. Inside the cover is a fascinating notice saying:

Christian Schools Cork
Premium
awarded to
Nicholas English
for success in
Junior Grade
of the

Intermediate Examinations

1885.

Countless poems have been inspired by love of place. Goldsmith is probably the master of these remembrances, and the theme of his poems is universal. How many generations of Irish people have been comforted by the words of Goldsmith who is surely our poet of place? His *Deserted Village* is a long, meandering poem and we learned bits of it at different stages throughout our school years, as did generations before us. A poet from the Irish midlands, Goldsmith writes of a world long gone, but his words have a soothing rhythm that are timeless and as comforting today as when first written. When my world goes topsy turvy and I am unable to concentrate on reading prose, then poetry is the solace, and it goes straight into the centre of my struggle.

The Deserted Village
Sweet Auburn! loveliest village of the plain,
Where health and plenty cheer'd the laboring swain,
Where smiling spring its earliest visit paid,
And parting summer's lingering blooms delay'd:
Dear lovely bowers of innocence and ease,
Seats of my youth, when every sport could please,
How often have I loiter'd o'er thy green,
Where humble happiness endear'd each scene!
How often have I paused on every charm,
The shelter'd cot, the cultivated farm,
The never-failing brook, the busy mill,
The decent church that topp'd the neighbouring hill,
The hawthorn bush, with seats beneath the shade,

For talking age and whispering lovers made!

How oft have I bless'd the coming day,

When toil remitting lent its turn to play,

And all the village train, from labour free,

Led up their sports beneath the spreading tree;

While many a pastime circled in the shade,

The young contending as the old survey'd;

And many a gambol frolick'd o'er the ground,

And sleight of art and feats of strength went round;

And still as each repeated pleasure tired,

Succeeding sports the mirthful band inspired;

The dancing pair that simply sought renown,

By holding out to tire each other down;

The swain, mistrustless of his smutted face,

While secret laughter titter'd round the place;

The bashful virgin's sidelong looks of love,

The matron's glance that would those looks reprove.

These were thy charms, sweet village! sports like these,

With sweet succession, taught e'en toil to please;

These round thy bowers their cheerful influence shed,

These were thy charms – but all these charms are fled.

Oliver Goldsmith

My father learned *The Deserted Village* in school and loved
to quote from it all his life, and indeed from many of the
other poems that he had also learned. I think those poems
enriched his life and deepened his appreciation of nature
and the land that he worked. In his time the school cur-

riculum was wide and varied and their far-seeing teacher introduced science subjects as well, so they experienced a broad spectrum of education. That generation of schoolchildren had no secondary-school education available to them, but the National Schools of the time had a seventh class and occasionally even an eighth class, and some of the teachers extended the lessons far beyond the curriculum. A good teacher can plant a seed that will germinate and blossom for a lifetime.

Maybe this is the reason that the section in *The Deserted Village* about the village schoolmaster clings to the minds of all who learned it in school. Would that we all had teachers like this one!

(The Village Schoolmaster) from The Deserted Village
Beside yon straggling fence that skirts the way,
With blossom'd furze unprofitably gay,
There, in his noisy mansion, skill'd to rule,
The village master taught his little school:
A man severe he was, and stern to view,
I knew him well, and every truant knew;
Well had the boding tremblers learn'd to trace
The day's disasters in his morning face;
Full well they laugh'd with counterfeited glee
At all his jokes, for many a joke had he:
Full well the busy whisper circling round,
Convey'd the dismal tidings when he frown'd:
Yet he was kind; or if severe in aught,

The love he bore to learning was in fault,
The village all declared how much he knew,
'Twas certain he could write, and cipher too;
Lands he could measure, terms and tides presage,
And e'en the story ran – that he could guage:
In arguing too, the parson own'd his skill,
For e'en though vanquish'd, he could argue still;
While words of learned length, and thundering sound,
Amazed the gazing rustics ranged around;
And still they gazed, and still the wonder grew
That one small head could carry all he knew.
But past is all his fame. The very spot
Where many a time he triumph'd, is forgot.

Oliver Goldsmith

These lines more than any others probably best capture the awe with which well-educated people were regarded by those for whom education was beyond reach.

Maybe as we are in *The Deserted Village* we should pay a visit to the village pastor? The majority of us in rural Ireland did not grow up with a village pastors but with a parish priest. Parish priests came in all shapes and sizes and with a huge diversity of personalities. It was a time when they wielded an unhealthy amount of power over their flocks. This turned some of them into control freaks, while others were kind and tolerant and walked in the footsteps of The Boss. Who a parish finished up with was all in the luck of the draw!

Before coming to live in Innishannon I had never encountered a Church of Ireland pastor and by the time I caught up with them they were known simply as 'clergymen'. The title 'pastor' had faded away, which in one sense, I think, was a bit of a pity as it had a certain old-world paternal flavour. In my home town of Newmarket we had a Church of Ireland church building, but not a resident pastor. A resident pastor or clergyman does make all the difference. Having a church with a clergyman is a bit like having a resident TD in the parish, it puts a human face on head office.

The clergyman in Innishannon when I came to live here in the early sixties was Rev. Matchette, who lived in the fine old rectory surrounded by a large garden at the western end of the village. The most obvious and delightful difference between him and the parish priest was that he had a wonderful wife. The fact that she was a splendid woman and a great addition to parish life was an additional bonus for him and us. That they were a very ecumenical couple further added to their widespread appeal. Mrs Matchette joined the local ICA (Irish Countrywomen's Association) and due to her position as a clergyman's wife was well accustomed to running parish events – she opened my young, inexperienced eyes to the diplomatic skills necessary to manoeuvre a smooth pathway through sometimes stormy parish waters. She was a sure-footed negotiator through tricky parochial problems. When she later decided to do bed-and-breakfast in the Rectory we got to know each other much better as I was engaged in the same business. She was a wonderfully kind, broad-minded woman, which led me to think that every clergyman should have someone like her to enrich and extend parish life. Rev. Matchette was a quick-thinking, impatient man, who enjoyed listening to classical music. When I told him that I thought this music might go a little over my head he patiently explained that you did not necessarily need to understand to enjoy, which put me thinking. He showed me many values. One day on calling to the rectory I found him stripping paint off the magnificent staircase thus revealing its beautiful natural wood. He was a man of many talents. They were a wonderful couple and would have been a boon to any parish and we were lucky in Innishannon to have them – as indeed were the people in *The Deserted Village* with their pastor, even though in this poem Goldsmith did not give the pastor's wife a look in. Sign of the times! Or maybe this particular pastor did not have a wife.

(The Village Pastor) from The Deserted Village
Near yonder copse, where once the garden smiled
And still where many a garden flower grows wild;
There, where a few torn shrubs the place disclose,
The village preacher's modest mansion rose.
A man he was to all the country dear,
And passing rich with forty pounds a year;
Remote from towns he ran his godly race,
Nor e'er had changed, nor wish'd to change, his place;
Unskilful he to fawn, or seek for power,

By doctrines fashion'd to the varying hour;
For other aims his heart had learnt to prize,
More bent to raise the wretched than to rise.
His house was known to all the vagrant train,
He chid their wanderings, but relieved their pain;
The long-remembered beggar was his guest,
Whose beard descending swept his aged breast;
The ruin'd spendthrift, now no longer proud,
Claimed kindred there, and had his claims allow'd.

Oliver Goldsmith

Chapter 17

To School through the Fields

Certain poems and stories awoke in us country children an awareness of the beauty that surrounded us, and lit up the world we lived in. One of the loveliest experiences of going to school through fields in the early morning was passing by sparkling spiders' webs on the hedges and furze bushes; they were also draped in misty veils along the tops of long grasses – and if you happened to be barefoot, as was often the case in summer, it was joyous to feel the warm moisture run down your legs and in between your toes. The miracle of the creation of these webs was beautifully described in one of our schoolbooks and this lesson is one of the many ways in which our schoolbooks enriched our appreciation of our way of life.

A Spinner of Silk

One of the commonest things in nature, yet one of the most wonderful, is the web of the ordinary garden spider. It is made entirely from silk thread, which she spins out of her own small body, and very skilfully made it is. You may see her busily at work on almost any evening in late summer or autumn.

Under her body are half-a-dozen spinnerets, or small spinning machines, each with a number of tiny tubes from which the thread is spun out. So fine is this silken thread that the lightest breath of air will make it float away, and yet it is stronger than a steel thread of the same thickness.

To start her web, the spider first of all makes the outside frame, by carrying the thread, or letting it float, from one fixed point to another on a bush or tree, working round in a circle till she is back to where she began. She goes over this frame again and again, adding layer upon layer of thread, till she knows it is strong enough to bear the web.

From the top of the frame to the bottom she now lets herself down by a thread which she spins out as she goes. At the bottom she pulls the thread tight with her foot, and fixes it to the frame with a tiny speck of gum. Any thread that is left over here she just swallows.

She runs back along this upright thread till she gets to the middle of it, and from this point she draws a number of threads outwards in all directions to meet the frame; they are like the spokes of a wheel. As each spoke is finished, she travels back along it to the centre of the web, and so out again with a fresh spoke.

Next, working out from the centre, she draws across the

spokes a spiral thread, which goes round and round, widening as it goes, till it reaches the frame. From there she draws another spiral, which keeps narrowing in till she reaches the centre again. It is these spiral threads, where they cross the spokes, that look like the steps of little ladders.

The web is now complete, and the spider has no more to do but retire to a corner and wait for her victim, the fly, to visit it. She will sometimes hide under a leaf near by, with a thread fixed to her foot and to the web. The trembling of this thread will tell her when a fly is caught. If her victim is too big and strong for her to manage easily, she will go round and round it with thread, tying it up before killing it.

Many people dislike the spider, because, they say, she is both cunning and cruel. But it must be remembered that she has no wings, and could therefore seldom catch her prey if she did not set a trap and lie in wait for it. Flies are the spider's natural food, and she plays her useful part in the world by keeping them down.

In Winifred Letts's poem 'A Soft Day' our early-morning world is beautifully captured and her poem also opened our eyes to the ingenuity of the industrious spiders who overnight wove their gossamer curtains over the fields.

A Soft Day
A soft day, thank God!
A wind from the south
With a honeyed mouth;
A scent of drenching leaves,

Briar and beech and lime,
White elder flower and thyme;
And the soaking grass smells sweet,
Crushed by my two bare feet,
While the rain drips,
Drips, drips, drips from the eaves.

A soft day, thank God !
And the hills wear a shroud
Of silver cloud;
The web the spider weaves
Is a glittering net;
The woodland path is wet,
And the soaking earth smells sweet
Under my two bare feet,
And the rain drips,
Drips, drips, drips from the leaves.

Winifred M. Letts

Poetry and lessons we learned in childhood wove a lining of awareness and attentiveness that opened our eyes and our minds, enriching our lives and extending our world into imaginary realms. This was very much so in the lesson about Narcissus, which totally captured my imagination and brought this young hunter into our fields and especially into the fairy well.

Narcissus

Narcissus was a young hunter who lived long ago in Greece. He had a beautiful sister whom he loved dearly. They spent all their time together, and were so much alike that people could not tell one from the other. They dressed alike, and both had bright yellow curls.

They were very fond of hunting, and Narcissus taught his sister to use the bow and arrow as well as he could use them himself. They spent many happy days together in the woods.

But one day the sister died, and Narcissus was left alone. He wandered sadly about, not caring for hunting now that he could not have his sister's company. He roamed through the woods, visiting all the spots he and she had loved best. He tried to make believe that she was still with him.

One morning soon after his sister's death he went to a clear spring for a drink. Kneeling upon the ground, he bent over the water. There for the first time in his life he saw his own face, reflected in the water. He did not know who it was, and thought that his wish had been granted and his sister had come back to him. He put his arms out to her, but the moment he touched the water the beautiful face in it was no longer there.

In dismay, he slowly withdrew to a short distance. The waters were soon smooth and mirror-like again. Then Narcissus went softly forward and again looked into the spring. There he saw the yellow curls and the lovely watching eyes looking up from the bottom of the spring. He spoke in soft, gentle tones, fearing that he might frighten her away again: 'Dear sister, do you not know me, your brother Narcissus? Speak to me, sister. Come, let us go to the woods together. I am so lonely without you.'

Her lips parted and moved as if answering him, but no

sound reached his ears. Narcissus stayed by the side of the spring all night and all the next day. He would sit and quietly watch the face in the water for a while, then he would try to coax the beautiful maiden, as he supposed it to be, to come out of the water and go to the woods with him.

For many days he lingered there without eating or drinking. At last he became too weak to watch any longer. His face became as white as the whitest lily, and his yellow hair fell over his hollow cheeks. His weary head drooped until it rested on the grassy bank, and there was no longer a face in the clear water.

The gods looked down in pity on the young hunter. They were so sorry for him that they changed him into a lovely white flower, which still grows beside streams of water. This flower is called Narcissus.

This lesson triggered off a huge curiosity in us about our reflections, and John O's well was our first source of investigation. John O lived in a little cottage beside the school and drew water from his small well that was tucked into the boundary ditch. On leaving school we galloped down this long hilly field, dancing around in large circles, flinging our school sacks up in the air. Free at last! But we all slowed down as we approached John O's well and gathered around it like thirsty calves looking for water. In front of his well John O had erected a tiny timber door to prevent his goat and the cows that grazed the field helping themselves to this pristine water that gurgled up from the bowels of the earth. If we forgot to close and firmly latch this little door we drew the wrath of John O down on us and he complained about us to the Master. Every day, on our way home from school we washed our milk bottles in John O's well and poured the rinsing water along the grass, not that we were aware of milk pollution, but rather we did not want to incur the ire of John O! When sparkling clean, we filled them from John O's well with ice-cold water to refresh us on the long meander home through the fields. When all the bottles were full, we helped ourselves to palmfuls of quivering water from the well. Then we waited for the water to settle down and took turns, like Narcissus, to admire our reflections in the well.

We had never seen Narcissus flowers, but this poem by Wordsworth made us aware of the dancing daffodils, with which we were more familiar. It has stayed with me all my life.

Daffodils
I wandered lonely as a cloud
That floats on high o'er vales and hills,
When all at once I saw a crowd,
A host, of golden daffodils;
Beside the lake, beneath the trees,
Fluttering and dancing in the breeze.

Continuous as the stars that shine
And twinkle on the Milky Way,
They stretched in never-ending line
Along the margin of a bay:

Ten thousand saw I at a glance,
Tossing their heads in sprightly dance.

The waves beside them danced; but they
Out-did the sparkling waves in glee:
A poet could not but be gay,
In such a jocund company:
I gazed – and gazed – but little thought
What wealth the show to me had brought:

For oft, when on my couch I lie
In vacant or in pensive mood,
They flash upon that inward eye
Which is the bliss of solitude;
And then my heart with pleasure fills,
And dances with the daffodils.

William Wordsworth

This poem by Wordsworth is a perennial that flowers every
year in our minds when we see the daffodils in spring. The
sight of them immediately brings Wordsworth's poem to
mind. But long before we see them, the daffodils and the
poem are rooted at the back of our minds, and in the cold,
bleak days of December and January when buds first begin
to peep up through the frost-hardened ground, the daffodils kindle hope in our hearts. As they slowly edge upwards
so do our hearts and spirits. They are the first encouraging
indication that spring is around the corner and they thaw

our frost-encrusted spirits. We watch them grow tall and elegant with the whitethorn hedges and when they begin to bloom this poem, that has grown with them in our minds, dances into our hearts inviting us to dance along with them. As children we loved to dance along beside the daffodils. What a precious gift Wordsworth gave us.

Chapter 18

A Wonderful World

Con once studied in a monastery and the following poem must have captured his imagination because he often quoted it and, from hearing the words over the years, the poem became familiar to me. It was written in the margin of a manuscript by an Irish monk working at Reichenau Abbey. I feel that the monk was enjoying the mental stimulation of his writing, and the comparison between his struggle with words and his cat's struggle with mice brings a smile to your face and paints a picture of the little drama going on beside him. It conjures up an interesting image of a monk with a quill in a bare cell wrestling and playing with words.

The Irish Student and His Cat
(This playful poem, translated into English verse, was written
    by an Irish student in a monastery in Austria.)

I and Pangur Bán, my cat,
'Tis a like task we are at:
Hunting mice is his delight,
Hunting words I sit all night.

Better far than praise of men
'Tis to sit with book and pen;
Pangur bears me no ill-will;
He, too, plies his simple skill.

'Tis a merry thing to see
At our tasks how glad are we,
When at home we sit and find
Entertainment to our mind.

Oftentimes a mouse will stray
In the hero Pangur's way;
Oftentimes my keen thought set
Takes a meaning in its net.

'Gainst the wall he sets his eye
Full and fierce and sharp and sly;
'Gainst the wall of knowledge I
All my little wisdom try.

When a mouse darts from its den,
O! how glad is Pangur then;
O! what gladness do I prove
When I solve the doubts I love.

So in peace our tasks we ply,
Pangur Bán, my cat, and I;
In our arts we find our bliss,
I have mine, and he has his.

Practice every day has made
Pangur perfect in his trade;
I get wisdom day and night,
Turning darkness into light.

Translated by Robin Flower

It is now interesting to learn from Con's old schoolbook that the poem was translated from the Gaelic by an Englishman, Robin Flower, a scholar who, on visiting the Blasket Islands, became completely enchanted with the culture and way of life of the islanders. He studied the Irish language and translated the works of the Blasket Island writer Tomás Ó Criomhthain into English. When he died his ashes were scattered on the Blaskets.

Living on islands and remote beautiful places stimulates the flow of creativity and anyone who has savoured the mystical essence of Gougane Barra where Saint Finbarr built his monastery in the sixth century will forever remember its peace and tranquility, so beautifully captured in this untitled poem about Gougane Barra that I learned at school.

There is a green island in lone Gougane Barra,
Where Allua of songs rushes forth like an arrow;
In deep-valleyed Desmond a thousand wild fountains,
Come down to that lake, from their home in the
    mountains.
There grows the wild ash; and a time-stricken willow
Looks chidingly down on the mirth of the billow,
As, like some gay child that sad monitor scorning,
It lightly laughs back to the laugh of the morning.

And its zone of dark hills – oh! to see them all
    brightening
When the tempest flings out its red banner of
    lightning,
And the waters come down, mid the thunder's deep
    rattle,
Like clans from the hills at the voice of the battle;
And brightly the fire-crested billows are gleaming,
And wildly from Maolagh the eagles are screaming:
Oh, where is the dwelling, in valley or highland,
So meet for a bard as this lone little island?

How oft, when the summer sun rested on Clara,
And lit the blue headland of sullen Ivara,
Have I sought thee, sweet spot, from my home by the
    ocean,

And trod all thy wilds with a minstrel's devotion,
And thought on the bards who, oft gathering together,
In the cleft of thy rocks, and the depth of thy heather,
Dwelt far from the foeman's dark bondage and
    slaughter,
As they raised their last song by the rush of thy water!

High sons of the lyre! oh, how proud was the feeling
To dream while alone through that solitude stealing;
Through loftier minstrels green Erin can number,
I alone waked the strain of her harp from its slumber,
And glean'd the gray legend that long had been
    sleeping,
Where oblivion's dull mist o'er its beauty was creeping.

James Joseph Callanan

Nowadays the little church at Gougane is a popular wedding venue and many people also make pilgrimages here to 'do the rounds' in the scenic lakeside grounds of the church to pray for family and friends who are ill.

Not far from Gougane Barra was the home of the Tailor and Ansty, a storytelling couple about whom Newry man Eric Cross wrote a book of the same name in the 1940s. The book brought the wrath of the Church and the rigid censorship board of the time down on all their heads in an Ireland not yet ready for such frank revelations. The book retells many of the Tailor and Ansty's stories, which were regarded as risqué at that time. The Church liked to control everything, especially sexual morality, and stories that came down from an ancient oral tradition did not tie in with such restrictions. It was an enormous scandal to the authorities that two ordinary people could think and talk like this! This harmless book is now part of our Irish culture – and I was delighted to find a copy up in the attic. Recently on a balmy summer evening a wonderful piece of theatre took place by the lakeside in Gougane Barra where the entire saga of the Taylor and Ansty was reenacted in a large theatre marquee before an appreciative audience. The spirits of the couple were probably in the audience quietly chuckling at the irony of the whole situation. They were free spirits, and maybe the following poem captures their freedom of being in harmony with nature.

The Wind that Shakes the Barley
There's music in my heart all day,
I hear it late and early,
It comes from fields are far away,
The wind that shakes the barley.

Above the uplands drenched with dew
The sky hangs soft and pearly,
An emerald world is listening to
The wind that shakes the barley.

Above the bluest mountain crest
The lark is singing rarely,

It rocks the singer into rest
The wind that shakes the barley.

Oh, still through summers and through springs
It calls me late and early.
Come home, come home, come home, it sings,
The wind that shakes the barley.

Katharine Tynan

This poem meant a lot to me because in the autumn before the harvest was brought in, our long Brake field was a glow of gold. The Brake was the bread-basket of the farm. Walking along the headland and looking up along the field, I was immersed in a sea of waving wonder. The wheat, the oats and the barley each had a different texture. The oats were a peroxide blonde and the wheat had the golden glow of the real deal, but the barley outshone them both because when the wind wafted through the field it gently lifted the barley's gleaming tresses that sighed in delight at the touch. A field of barley can talk to you and make you aware that we live in a wonderful world. When I first learned this poem I was immediately inside in that field of waving barley and my vivid, lived experience merged forever with the words of the poem.

I remember learning this next poem when I was very young. From an early age we were told to be careful not to get lost in these great big fields of corn, but this never happened because we travelled in convoy, the older ones looking after the younger ones. We often we sat on the ditch of

the Brake field from where we could look across the valley
at the Kerry mountains – this extended our sense of being
involved in a bigger picture and an awareness that though
very small we were still part of a wonderful world.

The Wonderful World
Great, wide, beautiful, wonderful world,
With the wonderful water round you curled,
And the wonderful grass upon your breast –
World, you are so beautifully dressed.

The wonderful air is over me,
And the wonderful wind is shaking the tree;
It walks on the water, and whirls the mills,
And talks to itself on the tops of the hills.

You friendly earth! how far do you go,
With the wheat fields that nod and the rivers that flow,
With cities, and gardens, and cliffs, and isles,
And people upon you for thousands of miles?

Ah! you are so great, and I am so small,
I tremble to think of you, world, at all,
And yet, when I said my prayers to-day,
A whisper inside me seemed to say!
'You are more than the earth, though you are such a dot:
You can love and think, and the earth can not.'

W.B. Rands

Chapter 19

A Terrible Beauty

One of my regrets in life is that I never mastered, or even got a modest handle on, the Irish language. I left school with no seeds of love for it growing within me, but that is really no excuse because I was given another opportunity of which I did not avail. My husband, Gabriel, had a great love and mastery of our language and would have been delighted to share it with me, but by the time he got to me I was beyond redemption. Sometimes when his efforts failed he would smile ruefully and tell me, 'I married a *Sasanach!*' (a Brit!). So my ignorant state continues and his wonderful old books in Irish are 'pearls cast before swine'; fortunately, one of our sons is following in Gabriel's footsteps and appreciates his books. So all is not lost!

But as a reluctant teenager the Irish words of the poem 'Mise Éire', by Pádraic Pearse, were emblazoned into my

Creóðan
Áileac
Tír Conaill

Airgialla
Ulaið
Dálnaraide

Dún Dealgan

Connacta
D Cruacni

Miðe
Áilun uinenen
Ecamair
Dunzascoi
Báile Áta Cliat
Breaillin

Inis
Laigin

Luimneac
Áileŋ

Muṁa
Caisel
Clioc Meala
Peatla
Loc Zarman

Corcac

z. Ó Murcaða

memory, never to be forgotten. The occasion was a St Patrick's night concert in our local hall when three of us teenagers, suitably attired in green and draped with national emblems, were lassoed into opening the performance with what was to be a stirring delivery of the poem. To say that I was terrified is putting it mildly. That terror had many strands, but the overriding one was that of forgetting my lines. So, for weeks in advance of the performance I repeated them all day, every day, last thing at night and first thing in the morning. I had no idea what the words meant, but knew that I was to deliver them in a ringing tone of the utmost conviction. My teacher told me that I was to imagine that I was the author of the poem. Now I blush with shame and humbly apologise to Pearse. But on reading about him recently I have discovered that his educational system was very child-orientated, so hopefully the teacher in him smiled in forgiveness at my ignorance and lack of appreciation. And for you who may, like me, not be blessed with a great knowledge of our native tongue, a translation follows.

Mise Éire
Mise Éire
Sinne mé ná an Chailleach Bhéarra.

Mór mo glóir
Mé a rug Cú Chulain chróga.

Mór mo náir:
Mo chlann féin a dhíol a máthair.

Mise Éire:
Uaigní mé ná an Chailleach Bhéarra.

Pádraic H. Pearse

This poem was extremely important in my school days and every child was expected to learn it. It was one of the few poems that I learned first in Irish and then later in English. Here's the English version.

I am Ireland:
I am older than the Old Woman of Beare.

Great my glory:
I that bore Cuchulainn the valiant.

Great my shame:
My own children sold their mother.

I am Ireland:
I am lonelier than the Old Woman of Beare.

Pádraic Pearse must be the most iconic figure in all Irish history as he was the leader of the 1916 Rising and its spokesman, with his wonderful abilities as a orator. To many he was a visionary revolutionary and a literary genius who changed the face of Ireland. To us, who grew up and went to school within living memory of the Rising of 1916, his dreams and writings coloured our landscape. When I read his story 'Eoinín na nÉan' (Eoineen of the Birds) at school I fell in love with his poetic idealism. His writing was so descriptive and detailed that I could picture Eoinín sadly saying goodbye to the swallows knowing that, due to his ill health, he would not be there to welcome them back the following spring. Running through Pearse's writing was an undercurrent of great sadness as if in anticipation of what was up ahead of him.

But for some, who like Gandhi believed in a national independence through a peaceful process, he was a bundle of contradictions. My father referred to him as the 'daft schoolmaster' who had caused havoc and led many to their deaths, whereas to my republican grandmother he was among the blessed. Uncle Jacky, who had been part of the 1916 upheaval and the subsequent civil war, seldom spoke of those days, almost as if they were too painful to remember. Jacky lived next door to us in Innishannon and we shared the same garden. There is an old expression: 'If you want to know me, come and live with me.' We practically lived together and he was a saintly, gentle man whom I loved dearly, and was as far removed from violence as you could possibly imagine. When he died I was surprised to find amongst his books a collection of the complete works of Pádraic Pearse, published in 1917 by The Phoenix Publishing Company. Those books, like all the other old books, were stored up in the attic. Our historical inheritance is complex and complicated.

In one of the old schoolbooks it was intriguing to find the following lesson obviously written by a student of Pearse in Scoil (Sgoil) Eanna, which was founded and run by Pearse in Rathfarnham, Dublin. From this piece we can see that he had a profound influence on his students.

Memories of a School

I remember the closing of Sgoil Eanna before Easter, 1916. I remember the Headmaster speaking quietly to the boys as they said good-bye. He knew it was the last time he would see most of them, but said no word out of the ordinary. He went on undisturbed with his work while the rumbling of the coming storm was audible to him alone.

Ah! such memories of Sgoil Eanna from its beginning! Its traditions are rooted in the first years, which have a glamour and a joyousness known only to the happy ones who shared them. From the first there was a question of something greater than a mere school, than the eternal rages of masters, mechanical programmes, and the pranks of boys. The miracle was achieved of making boys so love school that they hated to leave it. Every boy who came to Sgoil Eanna grew fond of it.

To take Ireland for granted – that was Pearse's own phrase to explain the spirit which filled staff and pupils. In athletics, in winning scholarships, in the everyday life of each boy, in the use of Irish as the official language, this spirit spoke in plain and appealing deeds.

Some enthusiasts will do anything in reason for the language but learn and speak it. Sgoil Eanna early removed that reproach by conducting the proceedings of the school committees in Irish. These committees had much to do with the running of the school, and were elected with great excitement annually by the boys themselves. One heard the different accents of the five provinces rising and blending in a splendid conflict upon anything from politics to minor details of hurling teams. Comparative newcomers soon followed the fray with a lively, intelligent interest.

No boy heard that English literature was a thing to be avoided; he did hear that Irish literature was one to be cherished and cultivated. No boy was forced to stop speaking English; he did hear Irish around him in all important school business, till he thought no more of asking why he should speak Irish than of inquiring why he should not speak Chinese.

What use, indeed, to write more in Sgoil Eanna's praise just now, or in praise of the things its Headmaster accomplished? Only those who have had the rare privilege of working with him there could understand aright. Some of us were with him in his last fight; we had seen the beginnings, strivings, adventures, and rejoicings of his greatest experiment.

'Pearse is the soul of this,' said one person while the Republican flag flew over Dublin buildings and the noblest thoroughfare in Europe mounted into ruins and ashes. While the street outside roared skywards in leaping and fantastic flames which made every cobble stone distinct, murmuring hideously and lapping the very clouds, inside a doomed building stood Pearse unmoved.

A cordon of soldiery were closing slowly in and around. The deafening riot of noise which rifles, machine guns, and artillery can produce rang in his ears. Upon him, of all men in Dublin, rested the weight of the huge adventure.

Staring unflinchingly at defeat, he walked the last from the darkened, resonant house of flame, down the bullet-swept streets, past the bodies that dotted them, past sombre alleys lighted by the flashes of machine guns, to the house where Connolly lay wounded. There he stayed until he walked thence to surrender and die, the old expression of pride and defiance in his eyes. It was the last glimpse men had of the Headmaster of Sgoil Eanna.

'The ideal of a dreamer, this college!' says some one. Oh! never believe it! In this system inspired by a lofty ideal room was found for such practical subjects as carpentry and gardening for boys, needlework and cooking for girls in the sister school Sgoil Ide, and ambulance and first aid for both boys and girls. And the boys and girls who were asked to be ready to emulate Emmet's or Anne Devlin's heroism were sent into the university and carried off first prizes in classics, or competed at the Feis Ceoil and were awarded gold medals.

Pearse had told us that the highest thing a man may do is serve. We, his students, have no greater praise for him than this: he showed us Ireland.

Desmond Ryan, The Story of Success

On reading through Uncle Jacky's copy of the works of Pearse, I came on 'The Rebel', a poem in which Pearse outlines his vision of things to come. This poem that I had never read before takes us into the revolutionary mind of Pearse. Reading it in view of all that happened afterwards is now a sobering experience.

The Rebel

I am come of the seed of the people, the
    people that sorrow,
That have no treasure but hope,
No riches laid up but a memory
Of an Ancient glory.
My mother bore me in bondage, in bondage
    my mother was born,
I am of the blood of serfs;
The children with whom I have played, the
    men and women with whom I have eaten,
Have had masters over them, have been
    under the lash of masters,
And, though gentle, have served churls;
The hands that have touched mine, the dear
    hands whose touch is familiar to me,
Have worn shameful manacles, have been
    bitten at the wrist by manacles,
Have grown hard with the manacles and the
    task-work of strangers,
I am flesh of the flesh of these lowly, I am
    bone of their bone,
I that have never submitted;
I that have a soul greater than the souls of
    my people's masters,
I that have vision and prophecy and the gift
    of fiery speech,

I that have spoken with God on the top of
    His holy hill.

And because I am of the people, I understand
    the people,
I am sorrowful with their sorrow, I am
    hungry with their desire:
My heart has been heavy with the grief of mothers,
My eyes have been wet with the tears of children,
I have yearned with old wistful men,
And laughed or cursed with young men;
Their shame is my shame, and I have
    reddened for it,
Reddened for that they have served, they
    who should be free,
Reddened for that they have gone in want,
    while others have been full,
Reddened for that they have walked in fear
    of lawyers and of their jailors
With their writs of summons and their handcuffs,
Men mean and cruel!
I could have borne stripes on my body
    rather than this shame of my people.

And now I speak, being full of vision;
I speak to my people, and I speak in my
    people's name to the masters of my people.
I say to my people that they are holy, that

they are august, despite their chains,

That they are greater than those that hold
them, and stronger and purer,

They they have but need of courage, and to
call on the name of their God,

God the unforgetting, the dear God that
loves the peoples

For whom He died naked, suffering shame.

And I say to my people's masters: Beware,

Beware of the thing that is coming, beware
of the risen people,

Who shall take what ye would not give.
Did ye think to conquer the people,

Or that Law is stronger than life and than
men's desire to be free?

We will try it out with you, ye that have
harried and held,

Ye that have bullied and bribed, tyrants, hypocrites,
liars!

Pádraic H. Pearse

I learned so much more about Pearse by revisiting him through Uncle Jacky's books from the attic. I had only had a smattering of knowledge about him and a very small appreciation of his thinking and his action. 'The Rebel' taught me so much about his ideas. It speaks volumes! This led me to search out the poem by W.B. Yeats about 1916, with which I was much more familiar, and I wondered how they would compare. It is from the same period. Pearse came from a different school of thought to Yeats, but the Yeats poem about 1916 gives us a great insight too into the thinking of the time and subsequent events. We have all been taught or heard of the following poem, but when I searched for it in the old schoolbooks it was not to be found. Then I remembered that many years ago, when I was buried in domesticity and business, I had bought a complete copy of the works of Yeats as a Christmas gift for myself. And so up to the attic again for a further search and there I eventually found it with the date of purchase, 1980, recorded on the cover. It was less pristine than when purchased as in the intervening years a splash from a glass of wine or a cup of tea had turned some of its pages to a soft amber.

Nevertheless, I hugged it like an old friend because there had been a period in my life when it was a close companion. And so amongst its pages I searched for the following poem and it took me a while to find it as I had thought that the poem was called 'A Terrible Beauty Is Born' as that is the line most familiar to all of us. But I had the wrong name as you can see.

Easter 1916
I have met them at close of day
Coming with vivid faces
From counter or desk among grey
Eighteenth-century houses.
I have passed with a nod of the head

Or polite meaningless words,
Or have lingered awhile and said
Polite meaningless words,
And thought before I had done
Of a mocking tale or a gibe
To please a companion
Around the fire at the club,
Being certain that they and I
But lived where motley is worn:
All changed, changed utterly:
A terrible beauty is born.

That woman's days were spent
In ignorant good-will,
Her nights in argument
Until her voice grew shrill.
What voice more sweet than hers
When, young and beautiful,
She rode to harriers?
This man had kept a school
And rode our wingèd horse;
This other his helper and friend
Was coming into his force;
He might have won fame in the end,
So sensitive his nature seemed,
So daring and sweet his thought.
This other man I had dreamed
A drunken, vainglorious lout.

He had done most bitter wrong
To some who are near my heart,
Yet I number him in the song;
He, too, has resigned his part
In the casual comedy;
He, too, has been changed in his turn,
Transformed utterly:
A terrible beauty is born.

Hearts with one purpose alone
Through summer and winter seem
Enchanted to a stone
To trouble the living stream.
The horse that comes from the road,
The rider, the birds that range
From cloud to tumbling cloud.
Minute by minute they change;
A shadow of cloud on the stream
Changes minute by minute;
A horse-hoof slides on the brim,
And a horse plashes within it;
The long-legged moor-hens dive,
And hens to moor-cocks call;
Minute by minute they live:
The stone's in the midst of all.

Too long a sacrifice
Can make a stone of the heart.
O when may it suffice?

That is Heaven's part, our part
To murmur name upon name,
As a mother names her child
When sleep at last has come
On limbs that had run wild.
What is it but nightfall?
No, no, not night but death;
Was it needless death after all?
For England may keep faith
For all that is done and said.
We know their dreams; enough
To know they dreamed and are dead;
And what if excess of love
Bewildered them till they died?
I write it out in verse —
MacDonagh and MacBride
And Connolly and Pearse
Now and in time to be,
Wherever green is worn,
Are changed, changed utterly:
A terrible beauty is born.

W. B. Yeats, written September 25th, 1916

I reflected on the two men: Pearse with his orator's energy
and ability to inspire people to revolutionary action, Yeats,
with the soul of a poet, able to acknowledge and contem-
plate an action he himself would never have undertaken —
one that he saw as both terrible and beautiful. How I wished
I had thought about this years ago and maybe I could have

talked about it all to Jacky – after all, he had lived through it and would have understood all the issues and contradictions.

My journey through the old schoolbooks has largely been one of remembering and revisiting, but I'm delighted to say that it has also been one of learning. Isn't it great how you always make new discoveries from books, no matter how familiar they are. Everything comes back into our minds, enhances our memories and opens up new avenues!

Chapter 20

What's in a Name?

My mother was not into quoting poetry but a poem by Wordsworth that she had learnt in school must have left a lasting impression on her. That poem was 'Lucy Grey' and it was lovely to listen to her quote the bits that she remembered. One of them was this:

> They followed from the snowy bank
> The footmarks, one by one,
> Into the middle of the plank,
> And further there were none!

Those few lines painted such a graphic picture that one would wonder about the whole story. I was very curious to hear the rest of that story, but my mother could only remember bits and pieces of it. Despite that, I developed a

big interest in the name Lucy Grey, even to such an extent as to wish that I had been christened Lucy rather than Alice! So from an early age I was fascinated by Wordsworth's Lucy.

In fact, one of his poems was the first that I willingly learned off by heart – I really *wanted* to do it. When I first came across it in school it rang a bell within me, and thus began a love affair with Wordsworth that has lasted all my life – though originally I had no idea who wrote it, as in school it was all about the poem, and the poet never got a look-in. At least, that's what I remember. But since the very first time that I read this poem I loved it and have got a lot of pleasure from simply reciting it to myself. Poems like this are golden stepping stones through life.

She Dwelt Among the Untrodden Ways
She dwelt among the untrodden ways
Beside the springs of Dove,
A Maid whom there was none to praise,
And very few to love:

A violet by a mossy stone
Half hidden from the eye!
–Fair as a star, when only one
Is shining in the sky.

She lived unknown, and few could know
When Lucy ceased to be;
But she is in her grave, and, oh
The difference to me!

William Wordsworth

We came across many of his works at school and when I realised that Wordsworth was the author of my mother's Lucy Gray as well as other beautiful poems, I so desperately wanted to read the full story of Lucy. I held this desire for a long time and did nothing about it, then suddenly one day at an auction in a grand old house near Mallow where they were selling off the contents, I went through the book lots and came on a box of books with a beautifully bound edition of collected works from Wordsworth. I waited for it to come up at the auction but there were some antique book collectors present that day and obviously this box must have contained some very valuable books. The price bids soared and Wordsworth floated away out of my reach. By sheer good luck I recognised the collector who had got my lot because at the time he occasionally wrote for one of the newspapers, always interesting articles. I had a vague idea of his address and on coming home wrote asking him if I could purchase the Wordsworth and, to cut a long story short, he called to me with the book and we hammered out a fair bargain. The result of his visit was that I had Wordsworth all to myself. Alleluia! And so for the first time since I had heard it as a child I sat down and enjoyed 'Lucy Grey'. Unfortunately my own Lucy poem was not in this collection, but that did not matter to me as I have it printed on my mind. But my mother's poem I had never read in its entirety and was so happy to have it at last.

Lucy Gray; or, Solitude
Oft had I heard of Lucy Gray:
And, when I crossed the wild,
I chanced to see at break of day
The solitary child.

No mate, no comrade Lucy knew;
She dwelt on a wide moor,
–The sweetest thing that ever grew
Beside a human door!

You yet may spy the fawn at play,
The hare upon the green;
But the sweet face of Lucy Gray
Will never more be seen.

'To-night will be a stormy night–
You to the town must go;
And take a lantern, Child, to light
Your mother through the snow.'

'That, father, will I gladly do!
'Tis scarcely afternoon–
The minster clock has just struck two,
And yonder is the moon.'

At this the Father raised his hook
And snapped a faggot band;

He plied his work – and Lucy took
The lantern in her hand.

Not blither is the mountain roe:
With many a wanton stroke
Her feet disperse the powdery snow,
That rises up like smoke.

The storm came on before its time:
She wandered up and down;
And many a hill did Lucy climb;
But never reached the town.

The wretched parents all that night
Went shouting far and wide;
But there was neither sound nor sight
To serve them for a guide.

At day-break on a hill they stood
That overlooked the moor;
And thence they saw the bridge of wood,
A furlong from their door.

And, turning homeward, now they cried,
'In heaven we all shall meet!'
When in the snow the mother spied
The print of Lucy's feet.

Then downward from the steep hill's edge
They tracked the footmarks small;
And through the broken hawthorn hedge,
And by the long stone wall:

And then an open field they crossed:
The marks were still the same;
They tracked them on, nor ever lost;
And to the bridge they came.

They followed from the snowy bank
The footmarks, one by one,
Into the middle of the plank;
And further there were none!

Yet some maintain that to this day
She is a living child;
That you may see sweet Lucy Gray
Upon the lonesome wild.

O'er rough and smooth she trips along,
And never looks behind;
And sings a solitary song
That whistles in the wind.

William Wordsworth

I finally had my Lucy Grey, the full story, and there was my
mother's verse third from the end. It was like an old friend

and it was wonderful to meet it in context. So, much to my satisfaction, Wordsworth joined my collection in the attic. Wordsworth's love of nature had enriched the lives of so many of us who learned his poems and they came back to us long after we had left school. Who would see a rainbow without this poem coming to mind?

> *Referring to the Period of Childhood*
> My heart leaps up when I behold
> A rainbow in the sky:
> So was it when my life began;
> So is it now I am a man;
> So be it when I shall grow old,
> Or let me die!
> The Child is father of the Man;
> And I could wish my days to be
> Bound each to each by natural piety.
>
> *William Wordsworth*

Wordsworth, like the Irish poet Katharine Tynan, was also intrigued by the cuckoo and this is another of his great poems that we learned in school. I could enter into this in a big way because of our enduring fascination with this bird, and the fact that Wordsworth called him a 'wandering voice' intrigued me. It was a bit like the cricket – the cuckoo was there and not there, a voice rather than a vision.

To the Cuckoo

O blithe New-comer! I have heard,
I hear thee and rejoice:
O Cuckoo! shall I call thee bird,
Or but a wandering voice?

While I am lying on the grass,
Thy loud note smites my ear!
From hill to hill it seems to pass,
At once far off, and near!

I hear thee babbling to the vale
Of sunshine and of flowers!
And unto me thou bring'st a tale
Of visionary hours.

Thrice welcome, darling of the Spring!
Even yet thou art to me
No bird, but an invisible thing,
A voice, a mystery;

The same whom in my school-boy days
I listened to; that cry
Which made me look a thousand ways
In bush, and tree, and sky.

To seek thee did I often rove
Through woods and on the green;

And thou wert still a hope, a love;
Still longed for, never seen!

And I can listen to thee yet;
Can lie upon the plain
And listen till I do beget
That golden time again.

O blessed Bird! the earth we pace
Again appears to be,
An unsubstantial, fairy place;
That is fit home for thee!

William Wordsworth

Thank you, Wordsworth! You enriched our lives.

Chapter 21

The Home Place

The house where we were born and grew up, be it a cottage or a castle, is the cradle of our formation. Wordsworth tells us 'the child is father of the man' and the Jesuit wisdom: 'Give me the child for the first seven years and I will show you the man' may well be true. And the words of Goldsmith may also apply: 'memory awakes with all its bushy train, swells in my breast and turn the past to pain'. But maybe the following poem is the one best remembered of all we learned at school. As children we all imagined our own homes when we learned this poem.

I Remember, I Remember

I remember, I remember,
The house where I was born,
The little window where the sun
Came peeping in at morn;
He never came a wink too soon,
Nor brought too long a day,
But now, I often wish the night
Had borne my breath away!

I remember, I remember,
The roses, red and white,
The vi'lets, and the lily-cups,
Those flowers made of light!
The lilacs where the robin built,
And where my brother set
The laburnum on his birthday—
The tree is living yet!

I remember, I remember,
Where I used to swing,
And thought the air must rush as fresh
To swallows on the wing;
My spirit flew in feathers then,
That is so heavy now,
And summer pools could hardly cool
The fever on my brow!

I remember, I remember,
The fir trees dark and high;
I used to think their slender tops
Were close against the sky:
It was a childish ignorance,
But now 'tis little joy
To know I'm farther off from heaven
Than when I was a boy.

Thomas Hood

Tragedy visited our home too, and also appeared in our schoolbooks. The death of a child must be the most heart-breaking experience that any family can endure. When I was six my little brother Connie, aged four, died of meningitis. At six you have very little grasp of the finality of death, but a few years later, on learning this poem in school, the baby in the cradle became Connie, and the poem was achingly sad. The picture of the men coming in from the fields was part of our farming world and we had a large wicker baby basket mounted on rockers under the stairs in the corner of the kitchen, where every day after dinner Connie was rocked to sleep. This poem repainted that picture for me.

A Cradle Song
O, men for the fields!
Come gently within,
Tread softly, softly,
O, men coming in.

Mavourneen is going
From me and from you,
Where Mary will fold him
With mantle of blue!

From reek of the smoke
And cold of the floor,
And the peering of things
Across the half-door.

O, men from the fields!
Soft, softly come thro',
Mary puts round him
Her mantle of blue.

Padraic Colum

But it can also be that the most ridiculous occasions of those years are remembered with a smile and, on reading a poem or a prose passage, a memory door swings open. Every Saturday morning we sisters washed and scrubbed the kitchen table and chairs. In our house and around the farmyard there was always a list of jobs to be done. I hated 'the jobs' and as a child thought that life without jobs would be heaven. However, on some occasions the jobs turned into a great 'tally ho!', and we had a lot of fun. To wash the kitchen table and chairs we drew water from the spout at the bottom of the yard and sloshed it all over the table and chairs. If the day happened to be warm and sunny we dragged the chairs down the yard and stood them into the water that flowed out of the spout and then into a stream along the bottom of the yard, to disappear in a little waterfall down into the fields. Standing barefoot in the water, we began the great wash and scrub. It was a free-for-all, with water being flung in all directions. Hopefully, at the end of the session, the chairs were a little bit cleaner. But after learning the following poem we almost expected the table and chairs to dance down the yard all by themselves!

The Table and the Chair
Said the Table to the Chair,
'You can hardly be aware,
'How I suffer from the heat,
'And from chilblains on my feet!
'If we took a little walk,
'We might have a little talk;
'Pray let us take the air,'
Said the Table to the Chair.

Said the Chair unto the Table,
'Now you *know* we are not able!
'How foolishly you talk,
'When you know we *cannot* walk!'
Said the Table, with a sigh,
'It can do harm to try,
'I've as many legs as you;
'Why can't we walk on two?'

So they both went slowly down,
And walked about the town
With a cheerful bumpy sound,
As they toddled round and round.
And everybody cried,
As they hastened to their side,
'See! the Table and the Chair
'Have come out to take the air!'

But in going down an alley
To a castle in the valley,
They completely lost their way,
And wandered all the day,
Till, to see them safely back,
They paid a Ducky-quack,
And a Beetle, and a Mouse,
Who took them to their house.

Then they whispered to each other,
'O delightful little brother!
'What a lovely walk we've taken!
'Let us dine on Beans and Bacon'
So the Ducky and the leetle
Browny-Mousy and the Beetle
Dined, and danced upon their heads
Till they toddled to their beds.

Edward Lear

However, our table and chairs were not as adventurous as the ones in the book and stubbornly remained clung to the kitchen floor and had to be dragged bumping and thumping every Saturday morning across the stony yard to be scrubbed. But that did not stop us visualising them waltzing up and down the yard!

In our house then, and probably in every home still, there lived a Mr Nobody. When we learned about Mr Nobody in our schoolbook he was the answer to our prayers!

Mr Nobody
I know a funny little man
As quiet as a mouse,
Who does the mischief that is done
In everybody's house!
There's no one ever sees his face,
Yet we all agree
That every plate we break was cracked
By Mr Nobody.

'Tis he who always tears our books
Who leaves the door ajar,
He pulls the buttons from our shirts,
And scatters pins afar;
The squeaking door will always squeak
For prithee, don't you see –
We leave the oiling to be done
By Mr Nobody.

Anonymous

But you never pulled that stunt on my sisters or you were firmly called to order and made to 'man up' and take the blame when you stepped out of line.

Tangled up in our memories are different faded scenes, happy and sad from the past. But to return to a ruin of what was once your home must be a very sad experience. A friend of mine loved painting old houses and one ruin she painted she christened 'Gone to America'. Emigrants travel long distances to stand on the land that once housed their ancestors. Then a few years ago I got a letter from a woman living in Dublin who, on visiting the ruin of a house miles away that her stonemason grandfather had built, fell in love with it. There was only the gable end wall of the old house standing on a small plot of land, but she withdrew all her savings and bought it. Her children thought she was crazy. But the poets would have understood.

Here he lies where he longed to be
Home is the sailor, home from the sea,
And the hunter home from the hill.

R.L. Stevenson

And, as a hare whom hounds and horns pursue,
Pants to the place from whence at first he flew,
I still had hopes, my long vexations past,
Here to return – and die at home at last.

Oliver Goldsmith

Here in Innishannon we have an old map of the village that has a very interesting story which I will try to keep as brief as possible because otherwise my editor will take lumps out of it or, worse still, judge it to be totally surplus to requirements! Innishannon, like so many other well-placed villages, was once owned by a landlord who created a map of the village and surrounding area to keep track of the rents which he deemed to be his due. This map has all the houses of the time numbered, with the names of the residents written down along the side. Unwittingly, he left us a little treasure trove. Though undated, we judged by the presence of one church built in 1829 and the absence of the other church built in 1856, that this map was created around the time of the famine. It has now been restored and is on the back wall of St Mary's church where it is sometimes viewed by returning emigrants looking for their ancestral roots. Before it graced the church wall it was in my keeping and it was heart-warming when people discovered their family name on it and sometimes even discovered the house where hundreds of years previously their forefathers had lived. It was often viewed through tears of joy! The home place really has a powerful pull on the emotions, and in this we are akin to the natural world where fish and bird life return to their ancestral natal beds to recreate themselves. We too are irresistibly drawn back to the place where our tribal roots originated to draw strength and resourcefulness from their ancient unplumbed depths.

So, now, having revisited and explored the books of my

childhood, I will wrap up with my own reflections on the home place in all our hearts.

Return
When I am drained within
And the light
Which leads me on
Is quenched,
I come to this place
To be healed:
Its serene depths
Reach out to me
In a warm embrace
And I know
That I have come back
To my own place.
I have lived my life
Far from here
But I have taken
This little place
In the walled garden
Of my heart
To rekindle my tranquility.
And when my life spring
Begins to fade
I make a pilgrimage
Back to my own place.

Chapter 22

The Battle of the Books

This book was excavated from a moth-eaten, tattered group of ragged old troubadours, overflowing with an assortment of poems and stories, an entertaining collection of old boys and dames in faded coats and torn jackets who came down from the attic. Buried within their motley depths were long-forgotten, hidden treasures.

But also hiding in there were fighting spirits that I had never anticipated and they were prepared to call me to order and stand up for their rights. These were tough, wise old birds who knew that they had buried jewels within and

they demanded I treat them with the respect they deserved. This brigade of tough old troopers proved to be mentally overwhelming and totally challenging. This had not been part of my plan!

I had thought of these old books as a collection of senile old dears well past their date of being productive members of society. But they did not think so! They had been awakened from their attic slumbers and now were ready to go into battle for the rights of their contents. And I was overwhelmed – there were just so many of them with so much to say for themselves. I couldn't get my head around it all. They had me in a state of utter confusion and flooded me in a tidal wave of self-doubt about my ability to take them on.

Just as I was about to admit defeat and abandon the struggle, a call came from my sister, Phil, she who had entrusted our mother's books to me: 'I'm glad that you have decided to do something with our old schoolbooks,' she announced. 'I was beginning to think that I might have given them to the wrong person.'

Huh! How would *she* like to be battling with these old soldiers? They had buried me in a bog of confusion and rendered me unsure of what to do with them. What was the matter with me? Or was it the books that were the problem? Over the years, on dipping into one or two of them up in the attic, they had cast a magical spell over me. Up there all was tranquil. But on bringing them downstairs they seemed to have lost their tranquility. And so had I.

Had the attic atmosphere added enchantment to their

allure? That attic for me was full of memories. Up there I had written my first book. The attic had been my haven and my bolt-hole at a time when downstairs was a frantic hive of activity, where one could not even think clearly, not to mention connecting with a manuscript. But when downstairs became a place of peace I moved down and began to write first in the Seomra Ciúin and then in the Curiosity Room, so christened due to its location on the village corner, affording a view of comings and goings from all sides.

Down here I wrote at an old oak desk that had been rescued from a junk shop where it had been covered in a hideous coat of black paint. I removed the dreadful coat with an evil-smelling paint stripper, almost poisoning myself in the process. But the old desk had responded beautifully to the subsequent french polishing, and with its many hidden alcoves and drawers absorbed all my accompanying requirements. It was a comfortable writing space. I was happy writing there, though it did take me quite a while to settle down in this new location.

Was it the same with the old books? Was their equilibrium disturbed by my bringing them down from the attic where they had lived happily for years and obviously felt comfortable and at peace? Medical experts inform us that moving house is high on the stress list. Maybe that was what was going on here with these old books. Had moving downstairs to this strange new environment unsettled them and brought out their warring spirits? We all know that we too can behave strangely when we are upset.

But enormous precautions had been taken to ease the stress of their move. Beside my desk was placed a much-loved antique table; this blond mahogany little gem was fit for the use of royal personages and on it had been laid these old books, ranging from the venerable to the ancient, with due respect for age. It was a fitting receptacle for the most fastidious. And, as an added bonus, attached to the elegant legs of this little table are wheels, so it could easily transport this precious cargo from the Curiosity Room into the Seomra Ciúin or the kitchen, should they or I require a change of scene – but I always put their feelings first, so they were being treated like royalty!

The plan was to do most of the work at the friendly desk in the Curiosity Room with the little table of books parked beside it. Did the old books not like this location? Maybe they preferred their quiet attic? Maybe this book should have been written up there. Maybe that was the problem with this motley crew? They wanted to be back up where they belonged. Down here they could not relax and be themselves. They were confused! I was confused and could not make up my mind where to begin. The old books were read and reread, decisions made and changed, conclusions reached and revised. The old books were behaving like contrary old lads and ladies, all seeking attention and had turned into a creche of demanding, geriatric toddlers. Maybe this book was not one of my brightest ideas!

And then came the breakthrough. The Kincora Reader stepped forth and took charge. 'Me first!' she proclaimed and promoted herself to leader of the pack. She saved the day and my sanity. All we had needed was a leader and, well, Kincora itself had been a major centre of power in ancient Ireland. So this was only proper order! We had a starting point. We finally got going. The philosophy that the longest journey begins with the first step became a reality.

But it was not all plain sailing. The overall approach to the book did not settle until, unexpectedly, magic came into play with the fairies, who wove their special spells and opened up enchanted passageways through the pages. It was a good start. Then old storytellers found peace and quiet beneath the great trees and the birds flew and sang through the branches, and they all poured forth their beautiful notes onto my pages. Then the poets came and sat beneath the trees where they recalled their tranquil and profound words.

Robert Louis Stevenson brought his sunny influence to bear and he who had forever remained a child at heart transformed the pages with his sense of wonder. Then, unexpectedly, Pearse appeared, he who before he became a revolutionary was a poet and a visionary, and had dreamt of a child-centred education system. It was not anticipated that he would play such a major role in this book, but then neither was there a plan to have such long encounters with Goldsmith and Wordsworth – Goldsmith, whose words of golden wisdom graced our minds long after we had left our schoolbooks behind; and Wordsworth, whose perceptive eye and poet's soul had coloured our young minds with indelible memories. Isn't it wonderful when a challenging beginning opens up eventually into new and unexpected channels? I now have a greater appreciation of the complexity of Pearse, and my love of Wordsworth and Goldsmith has grown. Then there's Katharine Tynan, a joyous rediscovery for me, she whose words absorbed the richness of her time and transplanted it into ours. I dwelt on her poems for a long time and they entered my heart at a new level. How much we owe them all! And these old troubadour books, the custodians of such treasures, they demanded attention – and they were right! They wanted it their way and I was guided by them. They led me to new and deeper understanding and appreciation of their contents. The old books took the lead and directed who was in and who was out. They dictated the pace, and harmony at last prevailed. The result is *Books from the Attic*. And I hope that you have met some old friends through the pages and enjoyed the reunion, and that you have made new friends too.

Now they have gone back up into the attic and are probably very happy to be back where they belong. They can rest now. They have done their job! I am very grateful to Mom, Gabriel and Con for preserving them all, and hopefully so are you.

The Books from the Attic

Thece are the books from which selections were made. Alice started school in the early 1940s, so they were published before then, and often many years before. The publication date is rarely given on the books and sometimes the publisher's name is missing.

The Educational Readers, Junior Book (The Educational Company)
The Kincora Readers, Preparatory
School and College Series, Fourth School Reader, Edited by Rev. T.A. Finlay, M.A., F.R.U.I. (Fallon & Co. Ltd 1905)
Land of Youth Readers, Junior, Intermediate, Senior (The Educational Company of Ireland, Limited)
The Irish-World Readers, Intermediate book
The Marian Readers, Junior (C.J. Fallon Limited, Dublin; Macmillan and Co, London)
Fallons New School Readers, Advanced Book (Fallon Brothers, Dublin)
Reading Time, Intermediate (The Educational Company of Ireland Limited)
A Child's Garden of Verses, Robert Louis Stevenson (Collins, London and Glasgow)
Goldsmith's Choice Works (W.P. Nimmo, Hay & Mitchell, 1884)
The Collected Poems of W.B. Yeats (Macmillan, 1933)
Poetical Works of Alfred Lord Tennyson
Collected Works of Pádraic H. Pearse (The Phoenix Publishing Co. Ltd., Dublin, Cork, Belfast)
Poems of William Wordsworth (George Routledge & Co., London 1859)